Fotografía Sellada y Firm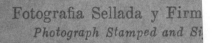
Photograph Stamped and Si

Sello
Ship's Stamp

Firma del tripulante
Signature of Member of Crew

Firma del Capitan
Signature of Captain

EXTRACT FROM ARGENTINE IMMIGRATION REGULATIONS

SHIP'S CREW.

Article 2.—Every sailor and member of the crew who figures on the crew list of a vessel which enters Argentine ports must be provided with a discharge book (libreta de navegacion) and an identity card (ficha) in duplicate bearing the photograph, which card shall be issued, signed and sealed by the master of the vessel.

Article 5.—No sailor nor member of the crew shall land from vessels arriving at Argentine ports until the master has handed in his identity card to the Directorate General of Immigration.

ME, TO NAME BUT A FEW

To Lili-Ann.

Happy birthday darling

Love John.

X X X

June 6/79

Also by Spike Mullins

RONNIE CORBETT'S SMALL MAN'S GUIDE
RONNIE IN THE CHAIR

Spike Mullins

Me, To Name But A Few

Foreword by Harry Secombe

M. and J. Hobbs
in association with
Michael Joseph

To Mary

First published in Great Britain in 1979
by M. and J. Hobbs, 25 Bridge Street,
Walton-on-Thames, Surrey and
Michael Joseph Limited, 52 Bedford Square,
London WC1.

ISBN 0 7181 1802 2

Filmset in Great Britain by
D.P. Media Limited, Hitchin, Hertfordshire
Printed by Hollen Street Press and
bound by Hunter & Foulis, Edinburgh

FOREWORD

A comedy writer is someone who puts words into a comedian's mouth. When they come out smoothly the audience thinks how clever the comedian is – when they come out not so smoothly the same comedian raises his arms in a gesture of despair. 'Who wrote this stuff?' he says, looking to the audience for absolution. The writer gets the blame and the comedian gets the applause.

Spike Mullins is about to redress the balance. He has written for most of the TV comics of the day and watched his work mauled by many – myself included. Now he has written a book which stands alone as a piece of writing without any comedian to muck it about. However, by allowing me to write the foreword to it he has failed to observe his own warning to his fellow scriptwriters – 'Never turn your back on a fully grown comic.'

His long blond hair and white beard could easily cause Spike to be mistaken for an Oxford don, until he opens his mouth and pours a pint of beer into it. I defy any professor – Cambridge or Oxford – to sink a pint as eloquently as he does.

As far as I am concerned he is the only person for whom I voluntarily gave up my lunch, and I can think of no greater sacrifice than that. I was playing Bridlington at the time – and losing – and decided one day to eat at a celebrated restaurant out in the country which had been highly recommended to me. On the way there I happened to switch on the radio and heard Spike being interviewed by Ray Moore. It was such an hysterical occasion that when I reached the hostelry I remained, crying with laughter, inside the car until the programme finished. I don't think I have ever laughed so much. When I finally tumbled out into the drizzling rain and staggered helplessly into the restaurant, the chef had gone home. But I didn't care.

When I read this book in manuscript I felt the same way, although I made sure bodily sustenance was at hand.

Spike is a delight to be with and his glorious disregard for the sacred cows of our profession is a joy. As a comedy writer he has to provide lip service for others, but he will never pay it himself.

I mustn't keep you any longer from the delights to follow. Read on, but be sure to order your next meal in advance.

Harry Secombe
October 1978

CHAPTER 1

The trickiest thing about writing an autobiography is not, as you may think, spelling autobiography, but finding a way to start the book so that whoever happens to look at page one will want to read page two and so on.

The night was cold and a light rain was falling, a few early morning market lorries trundled along Whitehall towards Covent Garden. Big Ben boomed three o'clock as a black limousine swept from nowhere and stopped at the kerb where I was shivering on the corner of Downing Street; a bearded face emerged from the interior and a cultured, high pitched voice said, 'The game's up Mullins, we've been tumbled, I'm off.' The car sped into the darkness in the direction of Buckingham Palace and that was the last I ever saw of King George V.

I bet that was the most intriguing opening anyone ever read in any autobiography and if there were any truth in it this book would have to sell a million. What a pity!

How about: The SS officer's features contorted with fury, 'Very well Engländer, if you will not tell us what we wish to know . . .' His finger tightened on the trigger of the great Luger, the muzzle an inch from my forehead. A nerve twitched uncontrollably in my cheek and I thought of England and Rupert Brooke's immortal lines, 'Stands the church clock at ten to

7

three? And is there honey still for tea?' Lies, more lies.

The only German who got a good look at me during World War Two was the occasional Luftwaffe pilot shooting up an RAF airfield, and then there was no dramatic confrontation about our meeting. All he would have seen of yours truly was a little blue-grey figure scuttling towards the nearest ditch, gasping, 'Please God I'll be a good boy and I won't pinch any more fags off the Naafi wagon or put any Waafs in the family way.'

No, for better or for worse you've got to tell it how it was and hope for the best, so here goes. The man fought me for the bone with a bit of meat on it and he cuffed me on my snotty little nose and I cried, then he took the bone and ran off behind the cardboard wall. And at the age of four I once again seriously considered how to get out of motion pictures.

Anyway the idea of a personal involvement in the early silent movies wasn't mine in the first place. I was at the time only four years old and I was such a puny child with so many ailments that I had more chance of becoming a laboratory specimen than a star of the silver screen, but we lived opposite the studios in the outskirts of South London and apparently whenever there was a part for a small boy that the audience would feel sorry for my mother used to wash me and cart me over there. And then they would dirty me up and make me cry.

My sister, who was two years older and a very pretty little girl, also got small parts. She was the one who had to point at me, and the caption read, 'Oh! Mummy, there's a dying boy on our doorstep.' So at the age of four I had more than half the family parasiting on the fact that I always looked as if whatever happened to me would probably be a merciful release.

My parents were an ill-matched couple, in fact so ill-matched that I sometimes wonder if they got married for a bet. Mother was a handsome woman who came from a family with a bit of property, and had a deep contempt for the 'little people' who worked for a living, and this included my father.

Father was a first generation Irish stevedore with a violent temper who was frightened of nobody and nothing except people in authority, and that included my mother. I remember they both had a favourite message for me when I was a kid. My mother would fix me with a steady eye and say, 'Hold your head up and look as though you belong to somebody.' And my father would keep his voice down and say, 'Don't upset your mother.'

Until I was about seven years old they kept the village sweetshop in the rural hamlet of Southend Village on the very outskirts of London where the trams turned round. But they were never very serious about shopkeeping and spent the profits in the Tiger's Head public house next door, until the shop went broke and Dad took himself off to America to make a new life for us all. But when he returned a year or so later it was apparent that he had spent his time in the USA as a hobo. So unless we were all going off to live in the hobo jungles outside the Chicago freight yards or ride the rods across the Rockies he really hadn't got a lot to offer.

During this period of time while Daddy was away carving his niche as a panhandler, my mother and sister and myself moved from lodging to lodging, most of the moves being caused by the fact that my mother was getting in a lot of the groundwork for becoming an alcoholic and was inclined to whoop it up a bit. I don't know where she got the money from but Mother never was one to discuss her private affairs with the kiddies, indeed such a question would have resulted in a clout round the earhole that would concentrate one's mind on more personal things like, 'Am I going to get my hearing back?'

I remember that by now we had been living for what seemed quite a long time in a large room in a lovely old house near Blackheath. The house was owned by a charming Jewish gentleman who had a housekeeper who sometimes gave my sister Kathleen and myself a hot meal when Mother was incapable of doing so. Then he would let us sit in his library where we spent hours looking at the coloured illustrations in his surgical text books. And he had a great rambling garden where my sister could pick his flowers and I could chase his chickens.

However this idyllic existence was soon ended with the return of my father, who lost no time in accusing our landlord of having an affair with my mother. The landlord immediately rallied a cohort of his finest tenants and we were thrown out of there, as they say, like a penny to an organ grinder.

And so we moved to Greenwich to be nearer the docks so that my father could resume his original calling as a stevedore. In Greenwich we rented two upstairs rooms in the house of a Mrs Beams, a crippled old widow lady with beady eyes and a sharp tongue and an allergy towards noise. Her only joy in life was her weedy twenty-year-old son who, when he wasn't busy with the housework, spent all his time dancing the Charleston in his patent leather winkle-picker shoes. My father, fresh back from his conquest of Chicago and the Rocky Mountains and other such manly places, referred to the boy too loudly as a 'ponce' and nearly got us evicted before we were unpacked.

It was now that life began for me because I was allowed to go out and play in the streets with other boys. Up to this time I'd never enjoyed this freedom because my mother was of the firm opinion that any boy found on the street who was not on his way to or from school or the local off-licence was a 'gutter-snipe' and should be put down or sent to Borstal. But thanks to Mrs Beams's aversion to noise, the more time I spent out in the streets the happier everybody was.

I remember the bane of my parents' life in this respect was a boy I had become friends with called Arthur Condon who would insist that the only proper way to announce his arrival at our house was to push his dirty face against Mrs Beams's highly polished letter-box and emit a piercing yodel. This always caused Mrs Beams to have one of her 'turns' which she would pass on to her tenants in the form of a threatened eviction.

If one of my family happened to spot Arthur approaching the house from our window I used to be practically thrown down the stairs to open the door before he could sound off. But often by the time I had picked myself up it was too late and Mrs Beams was grabbing for the salvolatile and rehearsing her 'last warning' speech.

In the end my mother, a believer in the kindly approach if all else fails, called Arthur to her and explained the problem to him. Arthur gave to understand that he appreciated the situation perfectly, and his astuteness and cooperation earned him a queenly smile and a penny,

Next day we found he had dropped the yodel in favour of an ear-splitting screech that frightened even my father and caused Mrs Beams to have a 'turn' the likes of which she had never had before so that, pausing only to give us a week's notice, she passed away a few days later.

However, although poor Mrs Beams would not have appreciated it, the episode was not without its redeeming feature, because my mother's parents, hearing that we would soon be homeless again, took pity and bought for us a little three-bedroomed house in King George Street near Greenwich Park.

Moving into our very own house was one of those days like Christmas when everybody tries to see the likeable qualities in everybody else. Gifts were brought, drinks were drunk and smiles were smiled. But unbeknown to us there were others waiting to celebrate our arrival and when we went to bed that night we were attacked by armies of bedbugs. My father came home from work the next evening with what he described as the complete and simple answer to the problem, a package of sulphur candles, which he placed around the floors of the bedrooms, lit and returned downstairs again. Apparently he had omitted to read the instructions which state that all door jambs, etcetera should be sealed with tape. Soon the house was filled with the yellow acrid fumes of sulphur. The windows were opened. It was November, and we sat huddled round the kitchen fire and retched into one another's faces. Later, exhausted, we went to bed and coughed ourselves to sleep.

The sulphur candles, we found, had very little effect on the bugs except perhaps to weed out a few weaklings and thereby improve the strain. Thereafter my father took no action against them except to coat the walls occasionally with some powdered distemper which he bought in Woolworth. This he laughingly referred to as 'bug-blinding'. Whatever this treatment did it never blinded the little rascals sufficiently to prevent them finding one another long enough to breed. And we all lived together on unequal terms for quite a few years thereafter.

Perhaps having a home of their own again after all the ups and downs of the early years of their married life had a settling effect on my parents, because they now settled down to a period of what was to be the nearest to domestic bliss they were ever going to enjoy. My mother, except for the occasional lapse when the urge became too strong, stayed sober and cooked and made the beds and went shopping and ignored the neighbours.

My father went to work in the docks when there was any work, and when there wasn't he stayed at home and built fences and sheds and dug the garden and mended our boots. Actually he was about as good at mending boots as he was at bug control, and when you got your boots back with a thick piece of leather roughly the same shape as the original sole fixed on with hundreds of little brass nails, you practically had to learn to walk again. My sister used to hide her shoes so that he couldn't find them.

My father, incidentally, was the only man I ever knew who cut his own hair. He used to stand out in the garden on certain Sunday mornings with one mirror hanging on the corner of the chicken shed and another piece of mirror in one hand and a pair of scissors in the other. He invariably started off calmly whistling 'Maiden my maiden' from 'Frederica' through his teeth and within minutes would be red in the face, cursing and shouting, with his eyes standing out like chapel hat pegs. Somehow he never seemed to be able to reconcile himself to the fact that when you are looking in one mirror from another everything is sort of opposite, and one minute he would be snipping away delicately about four inches from the nearest hair and a moment later he would be hacking viciously at root level. But he always seemed fairly content with the result, and as he always wore a cap I suppose it didn't matter very much.

The reason my father went through this charade every few weeks was simply that he didn't like barbers, and this is one of the very few things I have in common with my father. I dread going into a barber's, always have done. It's the chat that gets me down. 'What d'you think of yesterday's game?' they say. What do I think of yesterday's game!? There is many an unweaned child could turn from his mother's breast and tell you more about professional football than I can. So I try to be one of the boys and I say something stupid and he thinks I'm an idiot and gives me an idiot's haircut. Or they say, 'Not working this morning? What's your line of business?' So I tell them I'm a scriptwriter and finish up apologizing for half the comedy output of British Television.

But whatever my father lacked in mending boots and cutting his hair he made up for in his ability as a thief. If he thought an unwatched object was worth anything and could be concealed about his person he would steal it.

14

Most of what he stole was taken from cargoes of ships that he was loading or unloading in the docks. My sister and I always knew when our father had brought something important home, because we would be sent out of the room while he divested himself of the loot. I don't know whether we were sent away so as not to be corrupted or whether they thought we were potential copper's narks. But whatever it was, he hated to come home empty handed.

I remember once he staggered into the house almost on the point of collapse because he had two small sacks of brown sugar, one on either side of his body under his overcoat suspended from a piece of rope that passed across the back of his neck. The sugar was raw and unrefined and not much good for putting in tea or anything because little bits of the Old Plantation floated on the surface, and you spent all your time skimming off or spitting out. So he decided he would make some toffee with it. He made the toffee in my mother's baking pans. And when it was finished and cooled off we all tasted it and it tasted exactly like brown sugar that had been burnt and mixed with road grit.

Then my mother complained that she couldn't get it all out of the baking tins when she went to throw it away. So he said, 'Jesus Christ, am I the only one who can do anything in this house?' And he took the tins out into the garden and bashed them flat with a hammer until they were no good for anything anymore. And my mother got very shirty. So he swore that that was the last time he was going to do anything for anybody and mother had to speak very sharply to him to get him in line again.

I remember a consignment of almonds that my sister and I munched until we were so ill that to this day neither of us can eat a piece of marzipan. Then the hundreds of sugary dried locust beans that he tipped out of his pockets for our delight one evening. The fact that you could get enough locust beans, if you liked them, for a ha'penny in the sweetshop to last you about two days meant nothing to him.

Once he unloaded from his pocket handfuls of a greyish flock material which he explained was raw asbestos which was impossible to burn, so he was going to make invincible everlasting lighter wicks from it. I was never considered a bright child, but it did occur even to me that as he only had one lighter there was no need for about half a pillow case full of the stuff, enough to make about a million billion lighter wicks. Especially as one everlasting wick would last him for ever.

Father spent the rest of the evening trying to make a lighter wick. But every time he tried to thread it through the little hole in his lighter it came apart and he had to start again. I don't know if he ever succeeded because all his moaning and groaning and heavy breathing gave my sister a fit of the giggles which she passed on to me and we were both sent to bed early.

Not everything that my father stole was inanimate. For instance the eel and the parrot. The eel he stole from the eel and pie shop in Deptford High Street when we were shopping one Saturday night. Deptford High Street on Saturday nights was a lovely, noisy, exciting place. The shops would be open until nine o'clock or more. The butchers', greengrocers' and fishmongers' shops were ablaze with lights, gas and electric, and the costermongers' barrows with hissing naphtha flares. The shopkeepers stood in their doorways or at their shop fronts and waved their arms, pointing and shouting hoarsely the virtues of the goods they had almost to give away because they wouldn't last till Monday.

When times were good we bought great bags full of shopping, meat and oranges and bananas and apples and cabbages and cod's roe and kippers, great bulging bags that cut your fingers, as much as you could carry. Then when the lights were going out and the tired costermongers began to wheel away their barrows we'd make our way to the Marquis of Granby public house, where my sister and I would be left in the doorway to look after the shopping while our parents went in for a drink, coming out at intervals with glasses of lemonade and arrowroot biscuits for us.

At closing time they would emerge, talking and laughing about something they had seen or something somebody had said, and we'd troop off down the street to the eel and pie shop. The eel and pie shop on a Saturday night was full of steam and lovely smells, and kids and people. We'd seat ourselves at one of the marble tables under the great mirrors on the walls, and while our parents consumed bowls full of hot stewed eels, my sister and I would put away plates of minced meat pies with lots of fluffy mashed potatoes all covered in the greeny grey parsley-dappled liquor that they stewed the eels in. And it didn't matter if you asked for too much and couldn't eat it all, my mother would laugh and say, 'I told you so, your eyes are bigger than your belly.'

The front window of the eel and pie shop was open to the world, and on the marble slab in the window were shallow zinc tanks full of bits of ice and live

17

writhing eels, graduated by their size: sixpence, a shilling, two shillings and half a crown.

It was one Saturday night after we'd gorged ourselves and were passing the window on our way home that my father dived his hand into one of the tanks and grabbed a large eel which he managed to stuff into his overcoat pocket when the man wasn't looking. All was well until we were seated on the tram going home, when the eel must have decided that he hadn't come all the way from the Sargasso Sea to spend the rest of his life in my father's pocket. He suddenly appeared, plopped on to the floor, and wriggled quickly off under the seats, which were crowded with passengers, and just as quickly my father was under the seats after him.

In a trice the tram was full of shouting, screaming, jumping people, some of whom had seen the eel and thought it was a snake and others who thought my father had gone berserk and was going to kill them all by biting their ankles off. Eventually my father emerged, red faced and breathless, holding his eel which by now was rather dusty and covered in old tram tickets.

When the people saw what the situation was they started to laugh about it, all except the conductor who kept saying that my father had no right to bring an eel on his tram. But my father just stuffed the eel back into his pocket and asked the conductor if he wanted a knuckle sandwich. And the man said, no, he didn't want anything like that. So father said, 'Well, that's all right then.' And we continued our journey without further incident.

When we got off the tram my mother said she was pleased with father for not actually starting any trouble, but if he thought she was going to cook that poor eel which had been kicked all over the tram then he'd better think again. My father paused under the next lamppost and held the now very subdued eel up for inspection, and said, 'No, he don't look as fresh as he did, does he?' Then he shouted, 'Room for one more upstairs!' like the bus conductors do, tossed the eel through the upstairs open window of the house opposite, picked up his shopping and skipped off down the street, and we had to run after him. My mother pretended to be annoyed but you could see she was laughing really.

The parrot was an Amazon green parrot, which he stole from a consignment of wild animals from South America. Of course it was no use sending us out of the room when Polly arrived, especially as she had got a good grip on his finger where he was holding her under his coat, and as soon as he got indoors the air was blue with his profanity and her squawks and screams as he tried to make her let go.

As the parrot had come from South America my father presumed that she could speak Spanish and he tied her by her leg with a piece of string to the back of a chair and kept shouting 'Hispaniola' at her. Whether she had ever learned to talk or not, being maltreated and shouted at by a bad-tempered Cockney Irishman certainly didn't unlock the floodgates of her vocabulary, and apart from that clicking noise that parrots make she remained very silent indeed.

Later that evening he took the parrot along the road to The Woodman public house where he said the publican would give him a handsome sum of money for her. Whether or not the publican ever had any ambition to become the owner of a stolen Amazon green parrot what happened next must have put him off the idea once and for all. Because my father perched the parrot on a rail above the counter and everyone fed her peanuts until someone announced that she had relieved herself in his beer, and my father, taking this as a personal affront on his new found friend, started a fight, the outcome of which was that Jeremiah Mullins and Polly Parrot returned home that evening very much the worse for wear. And while such goings-on were the breath of life to my father, the parrot who had been brought up in the jungle found the excitement too much and died the following day.

I don't recall my father ever showing anything more than a cursory interest in me as a child, in fact as I remember I was never much more than someone to be shod, shouted at and sent to bed. Therefore it surprised me one evening when he came home and said that he had that day been working on one of the last of the great sailing ships, the Herzogin Cecile, and that he would take me to the East India Dock on the morrow, so that one day I could say that I had actually been aboard such a vessel.

Personally the thought of a day out with my father thrilled me less than somewhat, but the consequences of declining such a thoughtful gesture might be fraught with peril, so early next morning, in silence and side by side, we made our way to the East India Dock.

The Herzogin Cecile impressed me hardly at all. All I could see was a boat with a lot of masts and spars and men and ropes all over her. And my father was, as usual, very disappointed in me and gave me my fare home and went into a dockside pub probably to try to forget about me.

And there the memory would have ended and is hardly worth the mention, except that a few years later when I was about seventeen I happened to be standing on the deck of a tramp steamer on her way to the Bristol Channel when somebody shouted, 'Look over there, there's a big sailing ship on the rocks!'

And somebody else said, 'Blimey, you don't see many of them about. Who is she?'

And somebody went and got a pair of binoculars and said, 'She's the *Herzogin Cecile*.'

And someone said, 'Never heard of her.'

And I said, 'Oh yes, she's one of the last of the four-masted barques.'

'How do you know?'

'I've been aboard her.'

And the bosun said, 'You lying bastard, go and get on with your work.'

We kids went to the local council school, where I recall there were about a dozen boys who were considered by the authorities so sub-standard as to require a free half pint of milk a day, and I was one of them. I remember that our spindly little band had to hurry to the boys' cloakroom at morning playtime where we would assemble silently in the gloomy undergrowth of hats and coats. Silent I suppose because each of us resented that he should be categorized with the others. There we would wait while a master came along to witness that we drank our milk and didn't pitch it down the sink, a gesture that would have done wonders for our morale, and, as we often guzzled from the same quart bottle, would have slightly shortened the odds of us catching TB off one another.

The only other demonstration of concern for our physical well-being was the occasional visit of a lady named Nitty Norah who used to sweep into the class room dressed as a nurse, and with a steel comb which she dipped into an enamel bowl of something would search our heads for signs of wildlife. I remember she had a knack of grabbing you by the fleshy part of the face prior to lacerating your scalp, and when you staggered away it took about ten minutes to get your jaw working properly again. I also remember that she always said the same thing to the same kids, 'Tell your mother that if she doesn't do something I'll have to send you to the Cleansing Station.' And I for one had more important things to do than carry messages between Nitty Norah and my mother.

I nearly learned to play the violin when I was at Royal Hill London County Council School for Boys. It happened on a Monday morning. We stood in the hall, as we did every morning.

'Forgive us our trespasses,' we cried.

'Lead us not into temptation, Forever and ever, Amen.'

'Rock of ages cleft for me, let me hide myself in thee.'

'Pay attention now! Stop talking! Stop talking!' The headmaster, Mr Mills, had an obsession about people talking. I sometimes think it was his mission on earth to stamp out verbal communication among the human race.

'The next boy that utters a sound will go and fetch the cane from my study.'

We held our breath. Many of us would be caned during the coming week as we had been the previous weeks, but nine fifteen on Monday morning seemed an extra depressing time to start paying for our sins.

'That is better. Now the Country Holiday Fund

22

starts again this week, ask your mothers if you can come with us. If you want to come you will pay sixpence every week to Mr Jones. Do you all understand that? Stop talking.'

I never asked my mother if I could pay into the Country Holiday Fund. She might have said yes, and a week at Bexhill with Mr Mills and Co was the last thing I wanted.

'Now another item of news. How many of you would like to learn the violin?'

A sprinkling of hands shot up. Mine was not among them because not only did I not have any desire to play any musical instrument, but my brain was already bursting with the knowledge that King Alfred burnt the cakes and twelve twelves are a hundred and forty-four, and I had for some time felt that to burden it with any more was a risk that should not be lightly undertaken.

Mr Mills called me to him after assembly.

'Mullins, come here lad.' His tone was kindly and he laid a hand on my skinny shoulder.

'Now boy, wouldn't you like to learn to play the violin?'

At that moment, with that hand on my shoulder, the hand that had caned a thousand boys, to become a virtuoso on the violin seemed suddenly the only thing left in life.

'Yessir.'

'Then why didn't you put your hand up lad?'

'It's my mother sir, she doesn't like violins.'

'Nonsense boy, a violin is one of the loveliest sounds there is. I'll give you a letter to take to your mother when you go home tonight and we'll see, shall we?'

23

When my father had finished his dinner that evening my mother said, 'I've had a letter from Dennis's headmaster, He wants Dennis to learn the violin.'

My father looked at me crouched over the kitchen fire reading a comic and said, 'Well, I suppose as he is going to finish up in the gutter he might as well have something to do while he's there.' Perhaps the same thought had occurred to Mr Mills.

'It'll be a shilling a week for the violin and three-pence a lesson,' said my mother.

My father sighed. 'More bloody expense,' he groaned.

I would have loved to have told them that I didn't really want to have anything to do with violins and that Mr Mills had talked me into it. But I didn't trust either of them not to snitch on me, so I kept my mouth shut.

That violin was one of the most beautiful things that I had ever had. It lived in its black leatherette case and radiated warm and sensual tones of chestnut gold from its bed of virgin baize. And it smelt strange and sweet and cosy like memories of my mother's pillow.

The first time I took it home from school I walked the long way round so that more people would see me carrying it. Of course they looked at me. They had to, didn't they? I mean how often do you see a boy with a violin in a black, shiny, new, obviously expensive, leatherette covered case? You could walk down any street at any time and see a man with a horse or a lady with a pram or a kid with a scooter but not a boy with a violin, not in a month of Sundays would you see a boy with a violin.

Of course people didn't actually stand and stare.

Most of them pretended not to notice, either because they were jealous or they were too well brought up to embarrass me in such a way.

The coalman pretended to be busy putting the nosebag on his horse before going into The Woodman public bar, and even when I said, 'Hullo Coalman,' he hardly looked round from what he was doing until I passed by and couldn't see him. A group of neighbours outside the corner shop pretended to be talking about the price of eggs.

When I went into Mr Nunns the newsagent's, to enquire whether this week's Rover was in yet, he simply said, 'Can't you see it there on the counter, under your nose?'

And when I said, 'Well, I suppose I'd better take my violin home and come back for it,' he just replied, 'Please yourself lad,' and not what I imagine he was dying to say: 'Is that really your violin?' Or, 'I wish I had a violin like that.' Or, 'How rich and clever you must be to have a brand new violin.'

When I reached Joe the greengrocer's he had a few people in the shop waiting to be served. I said, 'Got any specky apples, Joe?'

He was weighing seven pounds of potatoes for an old lady and he said, 'Come back a bit later Dennis when I'm not so busy.'

'All right Joe, I'll just take my violin home, see you later.'

He looked up from clanking his weights on the scales.

'A violin, eh? Where d'you get that?'

I said, 'My mother bought it for me.'

He smiled. 'You going to give us a tune?'

I said, 'No, I can't really play it properly

yet; anyway if I take it out of the case it'll get dust on it and my mother will go mad.'

A couple of the customers smiled. I don't know what they were smiling at, perhaps they knew my mother.

I never did learn to play it though, because after the first few lessons the music teacher picked out the boys who were never likely to play the violin and I was at the top of the list. So that now, when one day I end up in the gutter as I probably will, I'll have nothing to do, which is really what I'm best suited for.

I do remember that we had our first wireless set about that time. It was a very impressive affair made by my mother's brother, Will. It had three large silver shiny valves and dials and coils, and on the shelf alongside a row of flat torch batteries and a squat glass accumulator which had to be taken, very carefully so as not to spill the acid, to the paper shop every week to be charged. It also had a very elegant loudspeaker with a curved neck like a swan, which crackled and howled and sometimes said it was time for Sir Hamilton Harty's Foundations of Music or that it was 2LO London and it was closing down.

Nobody was allowed to touch the wireless except my father. And when it wouldn't work, which was more often than not, he would pore over it, his breath whistling through the bristles of his nose, sometimes rearranging the row of four and a half volt batteries and reorganizing them with their little brass clips and occasionally muttering, 'I think it's me grid bias, it can't be me aerial, it might be me condenser.' These were the only wireless terms he knew and he used them liberally.

And nobody was allowed to speak to my father

26

when he was fixing the wireless; if anybody did speak to him he would invariably bang his fist on the shelf and shout, 'Jesus Christ all bloody mighty, can't you keep your mouth shut for five minutes? I nearly had it then.' Once I bounded into the room when he was fixing the wireless and asked if I could go to the pictures with Wally Lyons; he banged his fist down and the speaker suddenly said it was 'Carroll Gibbons coming to you from . . .' My father stood speechless for a moment, then snatched the plug out before Mr Gibbons could tell us where he was and shouted, 'Edie! When was the last time this boy had a bloody wash!?' Not willing to be party to a debate on that subject I turned and ran back to the street where I was safe.

That was the summertime of my childhood. I could romp with my friends in the long grass of Plumpudden Hill in Greenwich Park. Or play cricket in our street; the street was better for cricket, it was flatter and you didn't have to go so far for your dinner. Or I could lie on the warm felt on the roof of my father's chicken shed and read books and comics and eat lots of specky apples that Joe the greengrocer would sell me, about a dozen for a penny because they were unfit for human consumption.

I can hear now the brooding argument of the White Sussex hens and the nasal Cockney Irish American voice of my father as, from his chair in the kitchen doorway, he read in monotonous rising and falling tones from the News of the World to my mother as she prepared the Sunday dinner.

What a lot of Sundays we had then, and such marvellous weather up there in my little world of comics and apple cores.

In the *Boys' Magazine* I thrilled to the adventures of Falcon Swift, Master Detective, as, accompanied by his boy assistant whose name escapes me, he drove his great grey Hispano Suiza at breakneck speed through the midnight streets of Soho with a special green light flashing on the bonnet to show the policeman on point duty who was coming and presumably give him a chance to get out of the way.

I did admire Falcon Swift, a lean, monocled manhunter, who could shoot a knife from a villain's upraised hand, then with a lightning twist of his whipcord frame break another miscreant's arm with a cynical smile and a crack of splintered bones that would almost make me stop munching rotten apples.

But of all the people that lived in my comics I was devoted to Harry Wharton and his chums at Greyfriars School as they grinned their way cheerily through a fresh adventure in the *Magnet*, price twopence every Thursday. I would have given anything to be a member of the Remove at Greyfriars, whatever the Remove was. The fact that Harry Wharton and his chums were such terrible snobs, and saw the rest of humanity as 'villagers or townees' or 'cigarette smoking, card playing rotters, up to no good I'll be bound,' meant nothing to me, if anything I secretly admired them for it. And would have given anything to be on the receiving end of an icy glance from Mr Quelch MA, to hear him rap (he never spoke, he always rapped), 'Now cut along Mullins Major, cut along and do your prep.'

I was never quite sure what 'prep' was but if it was good enough for Harry and Co, it was good enough for me. I knew you did it in your study and if anybody knocked on the door you yelled, 'Clear off you awful bounder, I'm busy with my prep!' And then you opened a hamper of tuck that your mater very sportingly sent you before solving the mystery of what was going on between Jake Sneed, the village bookie, and Carruthers of the Sixth. What a lovely life!

I suppose, although I couldn't have explained it, what I really admired about Harry Wharton and his chums was their sophistication. Compared to them we were simpletons. Our idea of fulfilment was flicking cigarette cards against a wall, or running up and down the street with a piece of bread and jam in one hand while bowling a hoop with the other.

Saturday night was a bit special because the hot pie man came round, with his tricycle equipped with a paraffin stove selling hot paraffin flavoured meat pies. And those who could raise threepence bought one and those who couldn't said they weren't allowed them because they were made of dead cats.

Sometimes if it was raining you could go into the Baptist Mission where they showed coloured lantern slides of Jesus walking on the water. Or if it wasn't lantern slide night you could join the 'Band of Hope' and you'd have to promise not to go on the drink and then all sing a song called 'Give me sparkling water'; and if you didn't lark about they'd give you an orange and a certificate to show you were a lifelong teetotaller.

Sometimes if it was raining two or three of us would go round to Georgie Goodstone's house. Georgie Goodstone never had a father and his mother was a bit wrong in the head and used to talk to herself and stare a lot. The attraction about Georgie Goodstone's house was the mice. The Goodstones had mice like nothing you've ever seen. If you sat quiet in their kitchen for a few minutes, mice would come out from all over the place, hundreds of them, and his mother used to feed them bits of bread and talk to them. But after you'd been there about half an hour you'd had enough, the smell was a bit strong even for us. Somebody would say, 'Well, goodnight Mrs Goodstone.' And all the mice would flick back to where they came from. And his mother would stare at us as we filed out again. And if it was still raining we could go back to the mission and watch Jesus walking on the water.

Sometimes my mother's father would pay us a visit. He was a big fat frightening boozy man who owned property and bred Bulldogs and Alsatians. He would arrive out of the blue in a hired Crossley limousine complete with bottles of champagne and most of his present stock of Bulldogs and Alsatians. Then for the next couple of days the welkin would ring with the voices of my grandfather and my parents and the tinhorn gramophone, interrupted occasionally by a dogfight or a crash of glass and bottles as the horn fell off the gramophone.

Then the limousine would be sent for and they would all sing and shout and bark their way into it, never to return until they had perhaps quarrelled or been arrested. Sometimes I'd be at school when they left and the house would be cold, even in summer, smelling of dogs and cigars, and whisky and fish and chips, and the perfume of Californian Poppy, a scent my mother used in great quantities when she was drinking because she couldn't find time to wash.

Sometimes I'd cry a little because I was lonely, and then I'd search the debris for lost or forgotten money and sit and read a comic until my sister came home from Lammertons the draper's where she worked as an apprentice for seven and six a week.

My grandfather died when I was about twelve years old, that was my mother's father, the noisy one. My other grandfather, my father's father, was a little, quiet spoken Irishman who lived in Limehouse and believed in leprechauns. He was too nice and too poor to be of any interest and when he died I had a day off school to go to the funeral and I didn't go.

But we all went to my other grandfather's funeral and a grand day out it was to be sure. The cortège was about half a mile long with lots of flowers and lovely black horses and we wound our stately way around South London past properties and markets that he owned so that the shopkeepers and costermongers could doff their caps and shout, 'God bless you, Bill'. And then we all went back to where he used to live and everyone had a drop of sherry and cheered up a bit, especially my mother who learned that he had left her an annuity income so that for at least one month in every three she could live the life of an average well-to-do alcoholic.

Suddenly there weren't so many summer days. The chickens went and their roof fell in and I hardly noticed it.

Until I was fourteen I went to school and sat up straight and learned that A could empty a bath faster than B and all the red bits on the map belonged to the British Empire and Julius Caesar was murdered, and I walked home trying to avoid walking on the cracks on the pavement because if I walked on a crack it meant that Mum was on it again and the home would be empty.

Then there were times when it was hardly worth

avoiding the cracks because the front door had slammed before I was awake in the morning, when she had gone to Covent Garden Market or the Surrey Docks where the pubs open about six for the early morning drinks. I don't suppose when you think about it it was much fun for her being up and about so early. I used to wonder how she got there. Perhaps she had a friend who had a motor car. But that was doubtful because we never knew anyone who had a motor car, except my Uncle Ernie who lived in Biggin Hill, and I couldn't see him getting up before it was light to run my mother up the boozer.

The time came when it didn't really matter whether she was at home or not because when Mother wasn't drinking she used to be very tense and hard to get along with and she would have great purges about cleanliness and economy. And the sudden introduction of soap and water to a boy who sometimes went a week without a wash could be very distressing to say the least. At times it was like having Nitty Norah for a mother.

I remember that one of Mother's great economical gestures was in the culinary department. She used to make enormous bread puddings which were solid and grey and full of stony raisins, and these monsters would be kept in a wooden safe with a perforated zinc door which hung on the wall out in the yard. Sometimes the breakfast menu consisted of a cup of cocoa and a piece of bread pudding, 'To save wasting it and keep the cold out.' And in the winter a breakfast of cold bread pudding could be a traumatic experience, especially when you bit into it and came up against a lump of frozen suet the size of a walnut. One morning we had a difference of opinion about whether I was

**The Jeanette Macdonald and the
Nelson Eddy of the silent screen. My
sister and I.**

hungry enough to eat my frozen bread pudding, so she wrapped it in a piece of newspaper and made me take it with me. On the way to school I threw it at a boy named Charlie Thompson and it hurt his ear so much that his mother came up to the school next day and complained to the headmaster and I got the cane for it.

That food safe is strangely enough not only indelible in my memory for what it contained but for itself alone. A large solid structure, it jutted out from the outside wall facing the chicken shed above the drain, halfway between the back door and the outside toilet. And it was set at such a height that the wounds inflicted by it on my person in unguarded moments marked on my head the passing of the years from childhood to adolescence.

When I was small I walked under its jutting bulk until I could touch it with the top of my head standing on tiptoe. Then one day in headlong flight from my parents I found that I had grown an extra inch and received a bleeding scalp wound from the sharp corner of the door. From then on I received a lacerated forehead, a cut above the eye, until home from sea and slightly tipsy one night on a midnight journey to the outside toilet, I met it full face with an impact that brought both the safe and me to the ground with a clatter that set the dogs barking, the chickens squawking, and my father to his bedroom window, shouting, 'Jesus Christ, what's he doing now?'

To which I replied, 'Why don't you pipe down and go to bed!'

'What was that!?'

'I'm talking to the chickens!'

CHAPTER 2

For my first step into the great hurly-burly world of
commerce I took employment as an office boy to a Mr
Marks, importer of electric light bulbs, whose office/
warehouse was a sort of very large broom cupboard
high up in one of the buildings in Great Broad Street
in the City of London. The wages were twelve and
six a week, which doesn't sound a lot by today's
standards and wasn't all that much in those days
either.

When I reported for work that Monday morning my
parents had seen to it, to the best of their ability, that I
was suitably dressed for the great occasion. I had on a
pair of pinstripe trousers which retailed at four and
six a pair and were made in Poland from an ingenious
mixture of woodpulp and mutton cloth, and whose
principal fault was that after a shower of rain they
bagged at the knees and never went back, so that in
time you walked around with three knee caps on each
leg. My black city gent's jacket was purchased from
the Ladies' and Gentlemen's Secondhand Wardrobes
in Nelson Street, Greenwich and had been made in
Savile Row around the turn of the century for a fine
gentleman with good broad shoulders and unusually
short arms, the left even shorter than the right. Unfortunately I was a painfully thin boy with normal arms
but my mother said that I would 'grow into it'. The
ensemble was completed by a white cricket shirt,

34

black tie, a pair of brand new Admiralty surplus boots and a packet of fried egg sandwiches.

Looking back I think it is to Mr Marks's everlasting credit that when I clattered into his office that Monday morning, my almost white-blond hair plastered down with margarine and buckteeth gleaming, he didn't burst out laughing.

My duties were to spend half my time delivering parcels of our imports to various buildings in the city, and the other half trying to understand an ingenious filing system my employer had evolved, where all the green invoices went in numerical order with the green invoices and all the red ones with the red ones. Somehow I never seemed to master this part of the job, but if I felt anything at all about this inability I put it down to the fact that not once during all those years at the old Alma Mater had any mention been made of red or green invoices. And that I would reveal my full potential when someone wanted to know, 'Who burnt the cakes?' 'Whatever happened to Julius Caesar?' or 'What are A and B doing in the bathroom?'

Mr Marks was a large middle-aged man with a wealth of patience. He was also cross-eyed to the point where it was not funny anymore and suffered severely from bad breath. And he would sit with me at my little desk for long periods explaining the filing system. So that what with me and my reeking margarine-covered hair and him with his galloping halitosis we must have been well-nigh unapproachable.

But despite his physical shortcomings I was beginning to like Mr Marks, therefore it came as something of a disappointment when on about the Wednesday, during one of our filing lessons, he went an unusual colour and jumped to his feet, eyes going in all direc-

35

tions, and shouted, 'Jesus Christ, you bloody idiot, I might as well do this myself!'

I was, despite a certain resentment of his attitude, not sorry to be relieved of the clerical side of the business because it narrowed my personal commitment down to sweeping our office every morning and exploring London whilst delivering our light bulbs.

However it takes two to forgive and forget and while I was willing to resume our former amicable relationship Mr Marks was not, and withdrew into himself becoming surly and uncommunicative. And to my surprise there was worse to come. That Friday morning I was sitting on the floor in the corridor outside our office reading the *Rover* and eating one of the fried egg sandwiches while waiting for my partner to arrive, when a voice above me said, 'Mullins, I'm afraid you are not quite what I am looking for.'

Not at all sure what I was expected to say or do I gaped up at Mr Marks and some cold yolk ran on to my tie. He dropped an envelope into my lap. 'Go home,' he said, and unlocked his office, disappeared inside and slammed the door. The envelope contained my insurance cards and twelve and six which I put in the fruit machine in a café in Cheapside.

Then I went home and told my mother that Mr Marks had committed suicide and we wouldn't get any money until the Will was read and she tried to kill me with a Guinness bottle.

. . .The policeman on point duty looked down at me standing with my bunch of flowers, 'You've never had the pox, have you son?'

I was now a district messenger boy with a pill-box hat and a navy blue uniform with silver buttons and

36

was at that moment on my way to deliver the bunch of flowers to someone in the London Lock Hospital in Soho Square. I had merely said to the policeman, 'Please can you tell me the way to the London Lock Hospital?' To which he replied, 'You've never had the pox, have you son?'

'No sir,' I said, 'I don't think so.'

In my short life up to then I seemed to have had most of the ailments that flesh is heir to, but off-hand I could not recall any mention being made of the pox.

'Well, they've got it in there where you're going, every one of 'em.'

He stopped London's traffic and gave it a warning glance and started it again.

'Do you know what it does to you, son?'

'No sir.'

'It makes your doings drop off and you go blind.'

The thought of wandering about unable to see with no doings sent a thrill of horror through my silent frame.

'You'll see things in there that will be a lesson to you not to go with dirty women.'

I knew that was an unlikely possibility as only that week I had taken a personal vow to stay celibate until I could marry Joan Crawford. He waved some traffic away and stopped some more.

'Go down there, first on the left and you're in Soho Square,' he said. 'And be careful not to touch anything in that place. Off you go and don't forget what I told you.'

'No sir, thank you very much sir.'

When I got to the London Lock Hospital I shouldered my way through the swing doors taking care not to make contact with any of the woodwork with my bare hands, and crossed over to the reception desk keeping a watchful eye to see if I could see any of the terrible things that would be a lesson to me. The disappointingly normal looking lady at the desk took my flowers and signed my receipt. And it wasn't until I was on the bus going back to our base opposite Trafalgar Square that I realized that I *had* touched something, the little receipt that the lady signed on the wooden desk!

I took the piece of white paper gingerly from my pocket and dropped it on the floor and trod on it, then spat on my infected hands and rubbed them on the seat. The conductor saw me and said, 'What are you doing, you dirty little sod?' I could hardly tell him I was getting rid of the pox, so I said nothing and he chucked me off at the Haymarket.

I was with the District Messenger Company for quite a long time by my standards, about six weeks. Since leaving Mr Marks my average stay in any job had been about two weeks. Mostly one week to find out that I was unsuitable and a week's notice.

I'd been out in the world nearly two years by now and I'd had innumerable jobs, some more menial than others. Most employers seemed to want me to sweep things and clean things until I worked my way up. And as I didn't really want to work my way up and I had never personally cared about things being swept or cleaned, they soon found out their mistake and got rid of me.

Some employers did try to make something of me before showing me the door. Some of them tried fatherly kindness which I didn't understand because I wasn't used to it. And some tried shouting at me, but being shouted at was part of my way of life, so they might as well go shout down the nearest drain for all the effect they would have.

No, I wasn't very good at sweeping and cleaning, my forte seemed to be in delivering things. I could go from a given point and deliver something and return with a receipt with the same alacrity as the average fifteen going on sixteen year old with an average interest in shop windows, roadworks, and horses that fell down in the road, which meant you had to wait until the man from Harrison and Barbers came to shoot them.

In fact one of the best jobs I ever had was as delivery boy for a wholesale tobacco company in Farringdon Road, EC. My duty was to ride a box tricycle around the nooks and corners of London all day, and as long as I returned at the end of each day with an empty trike and a pocketful of receipts everybody was happy. Nobody ever said, 'Where the hell have you been?' or called me a scruffy bastard. This I felt, even when it was raining, was what God had made me for, to be a delivery boy with my own tricycle for dear old S. and A. Wholesale Tobacconist Ltd of Farringdon Road, EC.

But alas, even God was not to be trusted. Disaster fell one fine morning when I left the warehouse and pedalled my way happily up Farringdon Road heading for points west. An LMS wagon pulled by two great lively early morning horses thundered past and as was the custom among my ilk I grabbed a chain trailing from the tailboard and got myself a free tow up the road. My mistake came about when I twisted the chain around the little rail on the top of my trikebox and sat back arms folded and fell off.

In a moment the trike had turned over, and almost

39

before I was on my feet running and shouting to the driver, to be unheard above the sound of his horses' hooves and iron-shod wheels, the box was bumping and bouncing and busting Its guts all over the gleaming wet cobbles of Farringdon Road.

I was really crying when I staggered back into the warehouse with my arms laden with broken boxes of broken cigars and wet Balkan Sobranie, but nobody listened and I lost one of the best jobs I ever had.

Being a district messenger wasn't a bad job. You were supplied with a blue uniform with a little pill-box hat and a pair of boots and paid about fifteen shillings a week. Then you were hired out at I think about half a crown an hour to perform whatever task the hirer had in mind. You could be keeping some-one's place in a queue outside a theatre or you could be sent with a Christmas hamper to Oxford, or a lover would send you with some flowers to his lass at her flat in Mayfair, or she might send you with some flowers to him in the London Lock Hospital.

When we were waiting to be sent somewhere we were kept in a cellar underneath a theatre ticket agency on the Whitehall side of Trafalgar Square. The cellar was long and low, lit by an electric light bulb and a grating where the rain came in. The walls were dirty and the floor was concrete and always wet, and in the corner was a toilet with no seat and a gas stove where you could warm your dinner. There were also two trestle tables which were mostly used as football pitches in a game called 'Penny Ha'penny Football' which was played with twopence halfpenny and two combs.

It was in that cellar, often overpopulated as it was by twenty or thirty semi-unemployable adolescents

from the slums of London, that I discovered something about myself. I discovered suddenly on one
Monday morning that at the age of nearly sixteen I
was getting fed up with being pushed, and that,
skinny, buck-toothed and adenoidal as I am, if you
push me too much I will try to kill you.

The first to share this discovery with me was a lad
who, accidentally or otherwise, twice knocked my
comic off the trestle table making space for his tin
plate of dinner. With an alacrity that surprised both of
us, I'd hit him in the face with his dinner and opened
his skull with the edge of the plate, and was all set to
put him out of his misery with the wooden form he'd
been sitting on when he was rescued by some of his
friends.

He was a popular lad and as he disappeared up the
stairs on his way to be stitched at Charing Cross Hospital the biggest boy in the group, his ear swathed in
bandages because of a mastoid abscess, dug me in the
chest with his finger, 'Just as soon as this is better,
mate,' he indicated his poor ear, 'I'll bloody get you.'

That must have been one of the silliest things he
ever said, because as he turned away I managed two
good punches on the bad side of his head, and within
moments he was screeching his way up the stairs
with a handful of bandages and me after him bent on
further destruction.

The manager of the office rarely took any notice of
the occasional fracas among the boys, as such things
were fairly frequent and normally harmless, but two
hospital cases in one morning could not be brushed
aside so lightly. And I was sent for.

The manager eyed me up and down with distaste.
My baggy uniform was muddy at the knees where I'd

41

slipped while trying to administer the coup de grâce to one of my enemies, and I had two tunic buttons in my pocket.

'Well, 678, you are apparently a nasty vicious boy.'

He always talked to us as numbers because he didn't know our names and the number was on a piece of tin on the front of our pill-box.

'Who me, sir?'

'Yes, you sir, and I don't like nasty vicious boys. What don't I like 678?'

'Nasty vicious boys, sir.'

'And you are also a scruffy little bleeder, and I don't like scruffy little bleeders. What don't I like?'

'You don't like scruffy little bleeders, sir.'

We continued in this vein for a time, compiling a tedious catalogue of the reasons why he didn't like me, something that dismayed me not in the slightest; if my parents didn't like me I didn't see why he should. But on the other hand wild horses wouldn't have dragged such an utterance from me, as, along with most of my contemporaries, I had been brought up with an enormous respect for grown-ups, especially men grown-ups with tweed jackets and pipes who were probably doctors, insurance men or managers.

In the end we agreed, awful as I was, I was going to smarten myself up and behave myelf and I was going to make the most of my last chance. When I returned to the cellar it was all a bit quiet and one of the lads sitting with his mate on a form against the wall grinned and shouted, 'Oi, Niffnoff, did you get the sack?' I walked over to him and kicked him as hard as I could.

Later, the man sitting opposite me in the train from London Bridge to Greenwich looked at me and whistled. 'You've been in the wars, haven't you lad?'

'Yessir,' I said. My nose was still bleeding slightly, and looking down I could see the outline of my top lip and upwards the shadow of a still swelling eyebrow.

'Who did that to you?' he asked.

'Some boys sir,' I answered. I didn't want to talk because it was a bit painful and my left hand was throbbing in my pocket because somebody had bitten it.

'How many boys?' he asked.

'I don't know, sir.' And I didn't know, all I knew was that the boy I had kicked had started jumping about, obviously in great pain, and as I went in to give him the same again, somebody had said, 'Leave him alone!' And from then on I seemed to be fighting everybody in sight until I was rescued, and pushed out of the front door into Whitehall by the manager who told me that he would be writing to my mother. I don't know if he ever did write to my mother, she never mentioned it.

The house was empty when I got home. Still on the table were the odds and ends of breakfast, the half a loaf and the margarine, and the cold teapot, a bag of sugar, condensed milk tin and dirty cups. On the lino by the fireside chair were two empty Guinness bottles, and in the cold fireplace a dead mouse, his little anthracite eyes gazing sightlessly at a piece of Judas cheese, sprawled across a sixpenny mousetrap. A quick glance with a practised painful eye told me there was no forgotten money on the table, mantelpiece or dresser.

Then I wiped my face carefully on a wetted corner of the towel in the scullery and had a look at it in the mirror over the fireplace. Up to then of course I had had the usual schoolboy rough and tumble with the

43

usual cuts and bruises, but I'd never seen anything like this before, and I just hoped that when my friends saw me they wouldn't disregard my story of sending two kids to hospital and fighting God knows how many more, and put it all down to a road accident. Although luckily I still had the teeth marks on my hand, and by no stretch of the imagination is someone going to knock you down with a vehicle and then get out and try to bite your thumb off. And so, without further ado, I must away to Albert Merino's and recount my exploits to Albert, or better still to his lovely sister Maria, and any one of my friends who would be there to listen.

Albert Merino's was not really a caff in the true sense of the word. It used to be a caff but Albert's father had taken away the few tables and chairs because, as he told me and my friends at the time, 'I donta keepa da restroom for alla you layabouta sod.' You could still buy a cup of tea and a cheesecake although you had to stand up to eat it. And as Albert's father lived at his other café in far off Deptford and we were all young and fairly healthy lazy layabout sods it didn't worry us too much, we just layed about standing up.

Albert himself was born in this country and aged somewhere the other side of twenty. He was a big nice happy Italian; we used to argue that he was really English but he would have none of it. Albert Merino's sister Maria held, I'm sure, the proof of puberty to many of us. If you looked at Albert's sister Maria and nothing stirred, then you should have been at home playing with your box of soldiers, or seeking medical advice, because Maria Merino was sensational.

And Maria Merino knew she was sensational. She

44

knew that at the age of sixteen she had the loveliest face and the biggest eyes and the most gorgeous bosom and the tightest blouses in all Greenwich. And when Maria took over whenever Albert was away she sometimes carelessly forgot to do the top button up and when we bought something we would just as carelessly push a coin off the counter and she would bob down to retrieve it and you could see things that would make you feel dizzy. Oh Maria, Maria.

Just as old gold miners dreamt to find Eldorado, it was the young layabout's dream to push his clammy hand down the front of that blouse. And it was young handsome Georgie Waghorn who one afternoon, in a moment of friendly impetuosity, mentioned this fact to brother Albert. Still smiling Albert lifted the flap of the counter and taking the cake knife in one hand and Georgie's jacket front in the other pressed the knife edge against Georgie below the waist.

'If you ever mention my sister's name again I will castrate you,' he said.

There seemed to be some doubt as to what castrate actually meant, and as nobody wanted to ask Albert, I went next door and asked Joe the greengrocer, and when I told Georgie Waghorn the gory details, as per Joe the greengrocer, he nearly fainted, and he never said her name again. And I personally renewed my allegiance to Joan Crawford.

I never had much success with girls when I was a kid. Although I suppose success is relevant to your ambitions, which might range from a quick dive down the front of Maria Merino's blouse to a lifelong affair with a nymphomaniac lady publican, a resounding success as far as I was concerned would have been a ten minute conversation.

45

I never knew what to say to them. In a mixed group of boisterous laughing teenagers I was always the silent one, half smiling, enigmatic, aloof. And if it came to pairing up, the lucky girl who drew this man of mystery had got at least one surprise coming to her, because the more embarrassed I became over my inability to communicate the faster I would walk, and within minutes she would find herself whizzing round the block trying to keep up with a speechless idiot she'd never even met. And invariably after a couple of laps she would say, 'I've got to go home now to wash my hair.'

And I would brake slightly and say, 'Oh, I'll see you tomorrow night.'

And she would say, 'No, I don't come out Tuesdays.'

'Well I'll see you around.'

'Yes. Good night.'

'Good night.'

Sometimes I would feel like running after her and saying, 'Please don't go and we'll walk much slower and I'll try and say something to make you laugh.' But instead I'd give a shrug of feigned indifference and go back to Albert's caff and stare at Maria.

If I hadn't bumped into Bert Tracey that day I don't know what would have become of me. When you're sixteen and still writing to Joan Crawford you've got worries, especially when you never get an answer, and really it doesn't take six months just to write, 'Thank you for your letter, I love you too, Joan.'

Bert Tracey was about a year older than me, and lived just round the corner. I'd known him slightly at school but never liked him because he was clever. He won a scholarship and went on to the grammar

46

school. He worked at weekends in Joe the greengrocer's and was allowed to drive the coalman's
horse; to top it all he left the grammar school and ran
away to sea. How can you like a kid like that?

So I was walking past his house this morning when
who should come out but him.

'Hullo there, Blondie,' he said. 'How you doing?'

'All right,' I replied, and looked at him with a jaun-
diced eye. He was wearing the latest tailor-made full
length blue Melton overcoat with a white silk scarf
just showing at the neck, and a grey snapbrim trilby.
He looked all of nineteen or even twenty and the
spitting image of George Raft. I'd never really liked
him before, now I detested him.

He fell in beside me rolling slightly as he walked.
'Just got back from the Colonies,' he said, 'Aussie and
New Zealand through Panama up to New York and
back across the 'erring pond, Christ it blew all the way
across, bloody murder it was, never thought we'd
make it.' I nodded sympathetically and wished he
hadn't made it.

'Where you goin' now?' he asked.

'Nowhere special,' I replied, 'I'll probably have a
look in at Albert's caff, see who is about.'

He thought for a moment, 'Is that little Itie bird with
the big tits still there?' he asked.

I'd never hit anyone as well dressed and self-
assured as Bert and I didn't seem to quite know how
to start or even if it was such a good idea at all.
He continued unaware of his possible impending
doom.

'I had a Sheila down in Hobart last trip,' lapsing
into what I was to learn was an Australian accent.
'She was the spitting image of that little Itie bird, used

47

to creep into my cabin, couldn't wait to get her clothes off, lovely girl, can't remember her name.'

I looked at him incredulously. Here was a feller saying he'd been in a room with Marla's double with her clothes off and he couldn't even remember her name!

'Try pulling the other one,' I said. 'It's got bells on it,' tensing myself for the trouble I hoped would start. He gave a little laugh.

'I'm not kidding you, Blondie,' he said, 'they are all the same out there, can't wait for it, it's the heat. Come and have a drink, don't worry about money I've got plenty.' So saying he pulled from his fob pocket some notes including a couple of big white fivers and tucked them away again. I took a moment to get my breath back at the sight of such wealth, even my mother didn't have white fivers.

It was obvious that Bert was no stranger to the Red Lion. The barmaid was tall and beautiful with green eyes.

'Hullo Sailor, back again?' she said, as we entered the almost deserted public bar.

'Hullo Gorgeous,' said Bert, 'I've only come back to see you, give us a kiss.'

She leant across the bar and offered her cheek and he adroitly kissed her on the mouth. She drew back in mock indignation and looked at her lipstick in the back mirror by the spirit bottles.

'You are a saucy sod,' she said.

'Ah, leave off,' said Bert, 'you know you like it. Give us two pints of mild and what you want for yourself.' My dislike for Bert Tracey was by now rapidly turning into open-mouthed admiration. After all, who else did I know who went to Australia and made girls take their clothes off, *and* came back with riches

**My mother is in love with the camera,
but my father suspects the
photographer.**

beyond the dreams of avarice, *and* walked into pubs and kissed green-eyed barmaids?

We stayed in the Red Lion till closing time and had three or four pints of mild and a few games of darts, and once during an exchange of vulgar badinage Green Eyes said to Bert, 'It's a pity you're not more like your mate here, I like him, he's a nice quiet chap.' And to me, 'You don't go to sea, do you Blondie?'

Everyone does silly things when they are in love. So I said, 'Not yet, but I'm expecting to go next week.'

And she said, 'Oh well, come and see me before you leave, won't you.' And I knew I had to go to sea if only so that I could come and say goodbye to Green Eyes.

After we left the Red Lion we made our happy unsteady way up to Bert's house and sat in his front room and sang 'Buddy can you spare a dime,' until his mother got fed up with it and made me go home.

If this were a story book I could dismiss the very act of going away to sea so simply: Quickly I wrapped my belongings in the corner of a handkerchief, scribbled a note to Mummy, pinned it on the cat and made my way to the docks. The mate of the SS *Hernia* looked down at me, his weather-beaten face lapsed into a kindly smile as he placed his kindly weather-beaten hand on my curly little head, 'You'll do lad, stow your dunnage and turn in, we sail for Valparaiso with the morning tide.'

But it wasn't like that. I don't know how many days for how many weeks I walked those London Docks. I knew what I was going to be, I was going to be a galley boy. Because Bert Tracey had told me that the galley boy was the rottenest job on a ship and as I was unqualified and untried that was about the only job I was likely to get.

Each morning I set out rain or shine and made my calls at the dock offices of the shore superintendents of the various shipping lines. Knock! Knock! on the little hatch.

'Anything for a galley boy today, sir?'

'No, not today lad.'

'Can I leave my name, sir?'

'Christ, I've got your name about fourteen times. I'll let you know if anything turns up.'

'Thank you very much sir, good morning sir.'

The Blue Star Line, the Commonwealth and Dominion Line, the New Zealand Shipping Company, they all said almost the same thing every morning. These were terse hard gentlemen who had themselves been at sea most of their lives, and were not given to the niceties of conversation, at least not with would-be galley boys. Although there was one shore superintendent, Mr Hill of the Blue Star Line, whom I liked. He looked and talked something like W. C. Fields and he called me Joe.

Every morning I would knock on his hatch and the office girl would open it. And I would shout, 'Anything for a galley boy this morning, Mr Hill?'

And Mr Hill would look up from his desk and shout, 'Good morning Joe.'

'Good morning Mr Hill.'

'Nothing for you this morning, Joe.'

'Thank you very much Mr Hill, you've got my name, sir?'

'Yes, I've got your name, Joe.'

'I'll look in tomorrow, sir?'

'Yes, look in tomorrow, good boy Joe.'

Then off I would go to the Shipping Federation. The Shipping Federation was a sort of Labour

Exchange of the sea. It was situated somewhere in between the Victoria and Albert Dock and the King George V Dock. The aspect of the place was a very large dirty hall, empty save for some forms attached at intervals to the walls, the far wall from the door containing a sliding hatch through which the Shipping Federation officers made contact from their offices with the customers.

On a good day the Federation room would be crowded with smoking, spitting, shouting seamen seeking employment or waiting to sign articles preparatory to sailing. A practised eye could look around and tell with fair certainty to which part of the ship any member of this motley throng belonged. The stewards and members of the catering departments were the clean, neatly, sometimes fashionably, dressed groups with a proportion of effeminates and George Rafts. Bert Tracey was a steward.

The sailors were self-conscious in hard-wearing blue serge, mostly soft voiced, often Hebridean. And the firemen and trimmers would be capped and mufflered and noisy and laughing in Liverpool and Cockney. Sitting there on the form against the wall you could absorb fragmentary snippets of conversation, garnished with the names of exciting places, which would make you want to go to sea if you'd only come in to ask the right time.

'We was three bloody weeks anchored outside Mombasa.'

'When I joined her in New Orleans I didn't know she was going to Tokyo.'

'Don't talk to me about 'Frisco.'

'And you know what Santos is like, half the population has got the pox.'

I hope he didn't touch anything!

Sometimes the hatch would open and a man with a peak cap and a bit of gold braid on his cuffs would shout something like, 'Six firemen and four trimmers for the *Arandora Star!*'

Then there would be a little surge towards the hatch and someone might shout, 'Where's she bound for?'

And the officer would say, 'Brazil and the River Plate,' or, 'The Colonies.'

And someone would say, 'Sod that, I've had a gutful of down under, it's too bloody far.'

And somebody else, 'Aussie? That'll do me, be back for Christmas.'

I think I was waiting for the moment when the hatch would open and the man would shout, 'One galley boy for the SS *Somethingorother* bound for 'Frisco, Rio, Sydney, Mombasa and Tokyo and New York and never coming back again!' But of course it didn't happen like that.

It happened when one morning I knocked on Mr Hill's little hatch and I said, 'Anything for a galley boy this morning, Mr Hill?' And Mr Hill said, 'Are you going to let me down, Joe?'

I wasn't quite sure what he meant so I said, 'No sir, I'll be here every morning, sir.'

He got out of his chair and walked over to the hatch. I'd never seen him standing up and he was much bigger than I thought, and he wasn't nice and friendly anymore. He glared at me, 'If I put you on a ship will you spend all your time spewing your guts up and crying for your mum?'

'No sir, I won't do any of them sir, I can promise you that Mr Hill.' The girl started giggling. And he scratched his head thoughtfully.

'It's hard work, Joe.'

'I like hard work, sir.'

He thought for a moment, and then, 'All right Joe, but if you let me down I'll have your guts for garters.' And to the girl, 'I'll have yours as well if you don't stop that giggling. Give him a chit to go and have his medical.'

Oh dear! I didn't know you had to have a medical examination. I couldn't think off-hand what might be wrong with me but there must be something, even if it was the fact that I couldn't remember when I last had a bath.

'Right,' he said, 'take the chit over to Doctor Brown at Canning Town and get him to sign it, although I don't know why, he's always so pissed you could have an arm missing, he wouldn't notice it. He would have passed bloody Nelson A1 he would. You sign articles on board the *Avila Star* eleven o'clock tomorrow morning, galley boy, three pounds a month, and you sail on Friday, right Joe?'

'Right Mr Hill, thank you very much, sir.'

That was good news about Doctor Brown, wasn't it? I was nearly out of the door and going down the stairs when a thought struck me. I turned back and knocked on the hatch.

'What do you want, Joe?'

'Excuse me, sir, where are we bound for?' He swivelled his chair round and looked at a chart on the wall.

'Brazil and the River Plate. That's . . . er . . . Lisbon . . . Pernambuco . . . Santos . . . Porto Alegre . . . Rio de Janeiro . . . er . . . Rio Grande Sul . . . Bahia . . . Montevideo . . . and Buenos Aires, OK?'

'OK Mr Hill.'

'Good boy, Joe.'

CHAPTER 3

The *Avila Star* was a cargo ship of some ten thousand tons carrying a crew of about sixty officers and men. She was clean and well kept, with gleaming white paintwork and a single funnel with a big blue star painted on it. The galley, which apart from a tiny two-berth cabin below decks aft was the only part of the ship with which I was actually concerned, was situated in the superstructure amidships.

The galley was actually a rectangular iron box about twenty feet long and perhaps twelve feet wide, with two doors, one at either end so that in rough weather people could come and go by the door which left them in the lee of the superstructure.

Along one side of the galley was a massive black and, in some parts, burnished steel cooking range, heated by three coal fires. And on the opposite side wooden workbenches, a coal bunker, a large galvanized sink and a chute leading to the sea for putting the garbage down. The floor was made of brown Staffordshire tiles, and around the white painted walls were racks of saucepans and other cooking paraphernalia.

'And who the hell are you supposed to be?' The voice came from a thickset, hard looking, middle-aged man with hairy tattooed arms, wearing linen trousers checkered blue and white, big boots, and a white singlet stretched over a fat stomach.

I was sitting on my suitcase, smoking a Woodbine,

day-dreaming in the glow from one of the galley fires. I looked up at him. 'I'm the new galley boy,' I said. 'Who are you?'

He ignored my question. 'Get off your arse and don't ever smoke in my galley.'

I dogged the Woodbine and stood up. 'No, sir.'

He looked at me for a few moments as though I was part of an unpleasant joke that had been played on him.

'What's your name, boy?'

'Dennis Mullins, sir. The man on the gangway told me to come and wait in here.'

'Don't call me sir. Cook, that's my name, Cook, got it Dennis?'

'Yes Cook, is there anything you'd like me to do, Cook?'

'Yes there is, Dennis, I'd like you to get into your working gear and turn to, and clean this filthy hole up before we all get hydrophobia, and stop sitting around as if you was on your daddy's yacht.'

I suppose the biggest surprise in my new life was the discovery that my new masters were even more fanatical about cleaning things than were the old ones. I think I was surprised because I'd seen quite a lot of ships in the docks during my perambulations and they all looked very dirty and untidy, the decks littered with ropes and greasy steel hawsers and bits of cargo and peopled by scruffy, bawling stevedores; a panorama into which I must have felt I could blend as to the manner born as they say.

But as much as it offended my sensibilities there was no turning back, and by nightfall, goaded on by the cook and his assistant, a sullen twenty year old from the Channel Islands, I'd scrubbed my way out of

55

the King George V Dock and into the English Channel with hardly time to glance round to see what was happening.

Alone at last I perched on one of the snow-white benches and lit a cigarette. The lights of the coastal town glimmered in the distance and I wondered if it was Margate and if I could swim that far.

A passing stoker, black with coal-dust, his sweat-rag between his teeth, paused in the open doorway close to where I was sitting.

'Don't sit on that bench, Cookyboy,' he said, 'that's where our grub gets chopped up.' This, I thought, is too much. It's not enough that I have to put up with the cook and his mate moaning all day, but here is someone who doesn't even work in this department having a go at me.

'Listen, matey,' I said, 'if I can scrub it I can sit on it, so mind your own business.'

He put one grimy hand on the doorway and leaned inwards as if to impart some confidential bit of information, and as I leaned forward to listen to it he hit me a terrific backhander on the side of the head with the other hand which knocked me to the deck two yards away.

'Don't be saucy,' he said, and with a wag of his finger he disappeared.

Just as I picked myself up, the cook came into the galley.

'How are you getting on Dennis? All finished?' he asked.

I said, 'Here, d'you know what happened? One of those stokers just gave me a punch in the earhole!'

He stirred something that was simmering on the range. 'They will do,' he said. 'They will do.'

I went out on deck and had a long look at the dark water between me and Margate, and decided it was considerably more than a length of Greenwich Swimming Baths which was my all-time record to date, so there was nothing else to do but not be saucy and make the best of it.

Actually it was all right at sea once you got used to it. The day started at five thirty every morning, when, at the insistence of a sailor from the watch-on-deck, who often dripped water off his sou'wester on to my face on purpose, I fell from my bunk and made my bleary eyed way from the little cabin between decks that I shared with the assistant cook to the galley to stoke the fires and makes some mugs of tea for the cook and his assistant for when they started at six fifteen.

I also made a great enormous saucepan of porridge every morning, which the crew threw over the side every morning, because there was no sugar or milk to go with it, and in any case I wasn't very good at porridge and it was full of lumps. Eventually I suggested to the cook that as the crew only threw it over the side when they collected it in their dixies we should throw it overboard in bulk and sort of cut out the middleman; and he was so shocked at the suggestion that I am still waiting for an answer.

The days followed a fairly standard pattern. I washed all the saucepans and cooking utensils after every meal and then I scrubbed the galley and polished the brightwork on the range until, to quote the cook, 'It shines like a dollar on a blackman's arse.' Which along with, 'You're not on your daddy's yacht,' and, 'We'll all get hydrophobia,' was his favourite saying. And when I wasn't scrubbing and polishing I sat on deck and peeled sacks of potatoes. Sometimes while I peeled I'd think about my barmaid with the green eyes. I never did say goodbye to her. I went down the Red Lion one evening before we sailed but I didn't go inside, I admired her through a clear bit of the frosted window, the 'O' in Charringtons.

I'd dream about the day when, bronzed and weather-beaten and matured beyond my years by incredible experiences around the coasts of South America, I'd saunter into the spit and sawdust bar of the Red Lion. I'd order a pint of mild and she would serve me, but she wouldn't recognize me at first, probably because my voice had also changed. Then I'd casually light a long thin South American cigar and stick my thumbs in my snakeskin belt that I planned to buy in Rio, and I'd say, 'Well, don't you know me now?'

And suddenly those lovely green eyes would light up and she'd smile a beautiful smile, all white teeth and lipstick, and she'd sort of bite her bottom lip like Joan Crawford did when it'd all been a bit too much for her, and she'd say, 'It's been such a long time. Where have you been?'

And I'd say, 'Oh I've just got back from Brazil, and I thought I'd pop in.' I wouldn't say, 'Give us a kiss,' like Bert Tracey did, because this was a more special relationship and I wouldn't want her to think I'd become common like him. Then I'd give her a marvellous present that I intended to buy for her in South America. And after closing time I'd walk home with her and I probably wouldn't even try and kiss her goodnight because I didn't think she really liked that sort of thing.

But what they say about the best laid plans of mice

and men apparently also applies to galley boys. I never did see her again. Georgie Waghorn wrote to me that he'd been in the Red Lion and the missus had told him that the barmaid with the green eyes had 'pissed off with the guv'nor and all the loan club money.' I had already bought her a lovely picture made of butterflies' wings in Rio. So I gave it to my sister because when I got back she was in the TB sanatorium at Benenden.

When the weather was nice it was quite enjoyable sitting out there in the sunshine. You could watch the crew going about their daily tasks. Sometimes you'd see a whale or some porpoises and flying fish, or even the fin of a shark. On a good day it was almost as good as going to the zoo. When the porpoises were about, the best place to see them was up the front of the ship where they raced and criss-crossed the bow. And if the ship was pitching a bit you could sit with your legs either side of the flagpole and one moment you'd be rushing down to join them, then, as she lifted, surging skywards with your stomach trying to catch up with you. It was very exhilarating, but an officer caught me at it one day and told me that I'd get drowned and smashed to pieces, so I couldn't do it anymore. The day ended at about eight o'clock every night; there were no Saturdays and Sundays, if there were I never noticed them.

The cook and his mate and the stewards all went off to sleep in their bunks for a couple of hours every afternoon, but I very seldom caught up with my scrubbing and peeling sufficiently to follow them, so it was a very long day indeed. In fact I said to the cook one day, 'D'you know something? I've worked it out and I'm only getting about twopence an hour for all

59

this.' To which he replied, 'Well don't tell the owners, because it's a bloody sight more than you're worth and they might want some of it back when we dock in London.'

For about the first week at sea I ate and ate. I ate everything I could stuff down me. I ate even when I wasn't hungry. I gorged until I was uncomfortable with gorging. It got so the cook was saying things to his mate like, 'Don't throw that bucket of garbage over the side, give it to young scupperguts here, he'll put it under his pillow in case he wakes up in the night.'

But I wouldn't give him the satisfaction of knowing the secret of why I was beginning to take on the aspect of a pregnant broom handle. The reason was that I was following the only bit of advice that my father gave me before he nodded me goodbye.

'What you want to remember,' he said, 'is to eat as much as you can before you get into the Bay of Biscay, because it's always blowing in the Bay, seas forty feet high, so when you're seasick you've got plenty to bring up. There is nothing worse than being sick on an empty stomach.'

So about six days out I said to one of the ABs, 'What do they call this bit of water here?' indicating the flat blue expanse surrounding us.

'This, Cookyboy,' he replied, 'is what they call the South Atlantic Ocean.'

'Well when do we get to this Bay of Biscay?'

He thought for a moment, 'I should say roughly in about three and a half months' time.' I thought, Christ, have I got to keep this up for another three and a half months?

'That'll be on our way home again,' he continued. 'We came out of the Bay of Biscay on Thursday night.'

I said, 'My old man said there would be forty foot waves, I didn't see any forty foot waves.'

He nodded thoughtfully. 'He could have been right,' he said. 'You can never tell with the Bay, Cookyboy, you can never tell.'

I felt cheated somehow. Here I was stoked up for the biggest throw-up you've ever seen and it wasn't going to happen. A couple of days later we ran into a storm with waves forty feet high and I took no notice, if I couldn't be sick in the Bay of Biscay I wouldn't be sick at all.

Every morning after breakfast we all got brooms and lots of soft soap and scrubbed the galley floor and chucked buckets of hot water about to frighten the cockroaches, because at eleven o'clock the captain and his hangers-on, generally one of the mates and the chief steward and the bosun, came round the ship and inspected everything. They were an impressive sight, what with the gold braid and the brass buttons and everything, and when the captain stepped over the breakwater the cook came smartly to attention and saluted and said, 'Good morning, Captain!' and the captain saluted and said, 'Good morning, Chef!'

The first time I saw them do this I saluted as well, and said, 'Good morning, Captain.' But he didn't salute me and he didn't say good morning either. So when they'd gone the cook said, 'You don't salute the captain and you don't speak to him unless he speaks to you, remember that next time.'

I said, 'If I can't salute him why can you salute him?'

He said, 'Because I was in the Royal Navy and so was the captain.'

I said, 'Well you're not in the Royal Navy now, are you? So what's the difference?'

61

'Mind your own business, you saucy sod, and get on with your work.'

One morning when the captain came round he stopped and looked at me, where I was standing by the sink, and I thought for a moment he was going to say 'good morning' and I got ready to try another salute. But instead he said to the chief steward, 'Why doesn't this boy have his hair cut, Steward?'

And the chief steward looked at the cook, and the cook said, 'The bosun's mate has been busy, sir. I'll ask him to do it as soon as he can, sir.' That afternoon before the cook shuffled off to his bunk he told me to go up forward because the bosun's mate was doing haircuts.

The bosun's mate was like a lot of those Stornoway men that I used to see in the Shipping Federation. Soft of voice, big, blond-bearded and blue-eyed, he only needed a pair of cow's horns on his head and he could have been one of those Vikings that pillaged the Anglo-Saxons or someone when I was at school.

I found him sitting on the edge of number one hatch outside the fo'c'sle, a wooden stool was nearby, and chunks of other people's hair tumbled to and fro around the hatch in the breeze.

'You'll be wanting a haircut, laddie?'

'I suppose so, it's not my idea, it's the captain's.'

'Ay, he's a hard man, a hard man, sit you down on the stool.'

'I don't want it too short.' He began to scrape the bowl of his pipe with the scissors. 'I'd like it a bit like George Raft, parted down the middle, straight back and sort of straight across the neck.'

'This Mister Draft, he's a friend of yours?'

'George Raft, the film star.'

'Well now, I'm not at all sure that we can make you look like a fillum star, laddie, but sit you still and we'll do the best we can.'

I don't think that the bosun's mate had ever tried to actually cut anyone's hair to any sort of style before. Up to then, apparently, his idea of a haircut was to keep cutting until there wasn't enough left to make it worthwhile carrying on. And such was his reputation that anyone that had any respect for his appearance kept well clear of the bosun's mate.

But either because he was a nice man, or perhaps because he was intrigued by the challenge, he set to work to try to turn me into a practically albino George Raft. He snipped and clipped and combed, and sucked gurgling breaths through his empty pipe.

'Och, I think we're still a wee bit long on the port side there.'

Snip! Snip! Snip!

'Keep your head still, laddie, or we'll have the ears off you.' There seemed to be an awful lot of blond hair blowing around the deck.

'. . . Er, how're we doing, Jock, nearly finished?'

'Och, we're doing fine, laddie, just fine, square across the neck did you not say?'

Clip . . . Clip . . . Clip . . . Clip.

'My, but you've got an awful skinny neck for a fillum star.'

The four-to-eight watch of firemen and trimmers drifted out of the dark alleyway of the fo'c'sle and lounged on the hatch cover waiting for the signal to go to work. He stopped at last.

'There now, I think that's the best we can do for you, laddie.' And grasping my head with one enormous hand he swivelled it for the inspection of the stokers and trimmers.

'D'you not think the cookyboy here looks a bit like George Draft the fillum star?' The nearest of them eyed my head quizzically for a few moments. I knew inside me it had all gone wrong somehow.

'No,' said one of them. 'I think 'e looks more like George Draft the bleedin' 'edgehog.'

Gales of Cockney-Liverpool laughter swept the South Atlantic Ocean as they rolled about on the hatch choking on the phrase, 'George Draft the bleedin' 'edgehog.' As I walked away one of them called, 'Hey Spikey, what's for supper tonight?'

I said, 'Shit, the same as you always get!'

They convulsed again, and another shouted, 'That's right Spikey, you tell 'em, don't let 'em ride you Spikey boy.'

So 'Spikey' became Spike, and I didn't fight it because I'd always felt that 'Blondie' was a bit effeminate and to my mind anything was an improvement on Dennis.

At eleven o'clock the next morning the captain and his pals appeared as usual.

'Good morning, Captain.'

'Good morning, Chef.'

Salute! Salute!

'Everything all right, Chef?'

'Yes, sir.'

He looked at me and I looked at him. 'I see you've had the boy's hair cut, that's better.' And suddenly I realized what mutinies are made of. Up to then my favourite fantasy was me and Maria and Green Eyes in a big feather bed, but from now on I'd dream of the cook and Captain Jenkins RNR adrift in an open boat

64

My mother's parents—the original
Bonnie and Clyde?

with a big hole in it, saluting each other as they drowned.

When we were getting near to Brazil the cook started issuing dreadful warnings to me.

'I suppose you can't wait to get ashore in those whore shanties and get yourself a dose of the pox?'

'No, not really, Cook.'

'Well I'm warning you, boy, they've all got it, the whole country is rife with syphilis. D'you know what will happen to you if you get syphilis?'

'Yes I do.'

'Who told you, the chief steward?'

'No, a copper on point duty in Oxford Street about two years ago.'

'Don't get sarcastic with me, sonny, else you'll feel the toe of my boot up your backside. What will happen is that when you get a dose I'll send you to the bosun and he'll give you a chipping hammer and you'll work out on deck all the way home, and you won't be allowed to set foot inside this galley again.'

Suddenly even syphilis had its bright side.

'And you'll be disrated to a shilling a month.'

There's always a snag in everything.

Pernambuco was dusty and hot, and it smelt of sweat and cigars and bananas and mangoes. The stevedores were big, black and noisy and if I pointed at something and said, 'Very good,' they would point at something and say, 'Very good, mueta boa,' and I'd say, 'Mueta boa, very good.' And they'd laugh; already I can speak Portuguese.

'Mueta boa Brazilero!'

'Mueta boa Inglise!'

'Mueta obrigad!'

'Thank you very much!'

And the cook would growl and say, 'Don't waste your time gibbering with that lot, they'll put a knife in your ribs as soon as look at you,'

The cook was very unhappy whenever we were in port because it was always extra hot inside the galley, owing to there being no motion of the ship to make a breeze. The chief steward said to me, 'Keep an eye on old Cooky because sometimes he faints with the heat; if you see him going just help him out on deck and sit him down in the shade somewhere, he soon gets over it.'

The first morning in Pernambuco I was at the sink when the cook straightened up from putting something in the oven and he said, 'Oh dear, oh dear.' I could see he was about to pass out so I stood well back and he crashed on to the tiles nearly knocking his nose off on the oven door as he went past. I splashed a dixie of water over him and went and found the assistant cook and we carried him out on deck. He never fainted again the whole trip, so perhaps a broken nose is therapeutic for fainting fits.

I went ashore that night with the bosun's peggy. He was a Sunderland kid of about my age and he was also on his first trip to sea.

'Let's have a couple of beers and go up to the whore shanties just to have a look,' he said. I agreed immediately because I had intended to go up there anyway, only out of curiosity, because I didn't want to get a dose of the pox and spend the rest of the trip chipping rust off the decks for a shilling a month.

The street wasn't far from the docks, it never is. The doorways of the houses were made like horseboxes with the top half of the door open. Inside each door-way was a collection of maybe four or five half-dressed, laughing, chattering girls of pretty well every colour a girl can be. And I knew as soon as I glimpsed those lovely laughing faces that I had been misinformed about the possibility of catching something, because nobody could be as happy as this if she were afflicted by the awful things that everybody was warning me about.

' 'Allo jiggyjig? Sprechen de deutsch?' they said. They think I'm one of the Germans off the whaler!

'No sprechen de deutsch, me Inglise.'

' 'Allo Inglise, jiggyjig?'

Nobody ever walked along a street window-shopping like this. The further you strolled the more gorgeous they got. Two policemen in crumpled olive uniforms, armed to the teeth, with dark evil moustachioed faces straight out of 'Rustlers of the Rio Grande' in the *Wizard*, also strolled along. And for some reason or other if you stopped and leaned in the doorway for a few moments they bumped into you and growled, 'Vamos, vamos.'

' 'Allo Sailor, jiggyjig?'

'Me Inglise, how much? Muchas melries?' They seemed to like the Inglises, perhaps we got it cheaper than the others.

'Cinco melries – fife.' Five little brown fingers. 'Fife melries.' Let's see, a melrie is threepence, that's one and threepence.

'Vamos, vamos, vamos.' The half door opens, I'm in! And I'm up the stairs! And she was lovely and brown and naked and happy. And she bounced on the bed shouting, 'Jiggyjig! Jiggyjig!'

And when it was finished she said, 'Jiggyjig OK?' And I pulled on my clothes and counted five melries on to the little table and said, 'Yes, thank you, very good, mueta boa.' And as I went down the stairs I thought, 'Jesus Christ, is that what all the fuss is about?'

I found the bosun's peggy about an hour later. He was sitting at a table outside a café.

'Hullo there, how d'you make out?'

'All right, I did it twice.'

'I did it three times.'

'You bloody liar. D'you think we'll get the pox?'

'No of course we won't.'

Many members of the crew had their favourite ports in South America. And others, mostly the older members, hated every one of them. Some hardly went ashore at all, and then only to the Seamen's Mission, where you could have some free envelopes and paper and a quiet room to write to 'your loved ones at home'. But as my loved one at home had 'pissed off' with the guv'nor of the Red Lion and the loan club money I couldn't use the offer.

The ship's carpenter loved Rio. He'd been going to Brazil for years and years and every trip he blew everything he owned in Rio. He was middle-aged, of average height and weight and looks, in fact everywhere in the world he was average except in Rio de Janeiro; in Rio he was a prince.

As soon as the ship docked in Rio he was the first down the gangway, shaved and immaculate in sports jacket and flannels with cream cricket shirt and silk muffler. But from then on until about ten minutes before she sailed he became a roaring madman who was only ever seen in short glimpses standing up in the back of an open taxi, his hair on end, shirt unbuttoned to the waist, surrounded by bottles and girls,

68

singing loud unintelligible songs and shouting greetings to passers-by.

Then it was all over, he never went ashore again but stayed in his cabin and made model ships in bottles and wrote letters to his wife in Cardiff.

A lot of the crew who were living the high life were supplementing the few pounds they were able to sub off the captain with a bit of smuggling. Players Medium, Goldflake and Capstan cigarettes that could be bought on the ship for a shilling for fifty were always good for a few pesos or melries according to where you happened to be doing the deal.

But after the first excitement of reaching the coast most of the young bloods settled down a bit, and apart from purchasing beers and occasional souvenirs saved their money for the long stopover of about two weeks in Buenos Aires.

The assistant cook took me ashore in Rio and showed me the shops on the Avenda Rio Branca where I could buy my snakeskin belt and a picture made of butterflies.

He himself bought hundreds of little dead beetles. They were about as big as a lady's thumbnail, iridescent green and red ladybirds, beautiful and hard and brittle, with their little legs tucked neatly underneath just waiting to become a brooch. He told me he took some home every trip and the girls went mad about them. I didn't really believe that girls could go mad about dead beetles, and he gave me half a dozen that I casually offered to Maria Merino. The effect was amazing, and if I hadn't been so touchy about castration I'm sure I could have achieved my long-standing ambition regarding Maria's blouse buttons.

Buenos Aires was the turning-round point of the

trip. They didn't have brothels in Buenos Aires. But I wasn't sorry because we'd come a long way since Pernambuco and I was getting fed up with brothels. If you wanted to meet a girl in Buenos Aires you had to go to the part of town where the seamen's bars were. The Avalon Bar and the Splendid Bar and the First and Last and lots more of them.

There were plenty of girls in the bars, and if you fancied one of them you either took her to where she lived or to one of the local hotels which welcomed that type of guest. These hotels were very busy places, so they didn't exactly cater for residents. In fact, if you booked a room and you weren't out again in ten minutes somebody banged on the door and enquired, 'What the hell is going on in there!?'

The bars were exciting places, something like the old Wild West saloons that you see in the pictures. At night they were full of seamen and smoke and beer and whores. All the best bars had a brass band on a little stage, and when a few of you walked in during the early evening they would make a guess at your nationality and play what they thought might be your favourite national song, which could be anything from one of the latest talkies, 'Dancing cheek to cheek' or 'Lily of Laguna' or perhaps 'Red sails in the sunset'. Although they often guessed so wrong that you were saluted by perhaps a German or Swedish number you'd never heard of.

Surprisingly, considering the explosive mixture of girls and booze and men of all nationalities some of whom hadn't seen either for a long time, there was very little trouble in the bars.

Generally, if anyone did get a bit overcome by it all the waiters would form up and give him the bums rush, and that could be serious because it was said that, when they were on form, some of those waiters could throw a man clear across the road into the bar opposite. And you can guess what sort of welcome you got when you came flying through the doorway over there!

When the ship was in port we didn't work such long hours in the galley because the crew weren't on watches, so everybody had tea about five o'clock and we were finished for the day by six.

If you were too broke to go to town and you didn't fancy the Seamen's Mission there wasn't much to do. Although if you fancied a walk you could walk along past the abattoirs, where the frozen meat was coming from to go down the ship's hold, until you came to the railhead where the cattle trains came in from the interior.

Sometimes, if a train arrived while you were there, it could be exciting, because they put ramps against the trucks and the gauchos rode along on their ponies banging the sides of the trucks with their whips, and the steers came charging out in all directions, and if you got too close you might have to run for your life in a cloud of dust with the gauchos galloping and shouting and the steers bellowing behind you. But they didn't run very far, probably because they were stiff and tired and blinded by the sunlight. Then the cowboys herded them into great sheds and rode around them, whistling to quieten them down again.

One afternoon I went horse riding. The reason I had the afternoon off was that the chief steward came round and said that if anyone wanted to have any teeth out or filled they could take the time off to go up to town to this dentist, who was a friend of his and

71

who would do it all on the cheap. I suppose he was working his loaf for a free set of dentures or something.

As luck would have it I was in possession of a few pesos from the recent sale of my raincoat to one of the customs men who hung around the ship doing a lot of buying and selling of contraband and anything useful. So immediately I put myself down for a couple of extractions and fell to thinking how best to spend the afternoon, because I had no intention whatever of going anywhere near a dentist however cheap he might be.

'Why don't you come with us?' suggested one of the deck apprentices. 'We're going over to Quilmess to ride the horses.' The thought of riding a horse thrilled me about as much as going to the dentist's.

'No, I don't think I fancy that, thanks all the same.'

'Come on, it's a bit of fun, you don't know what you're missing, we do it every trip, it'll only cost you a couple of pesos.'

'No, I don't think so.'

'Perhaps you're frightened of horses?'

I never liked the apprentices because they had real uniforms with brass buttons, and they climbed the derricks and drove the winches, and stood on the fo'c'sle head when we were leaving port and shouted, 'All gone forward, sir!' and 'Steady as she goes!' while I was peeling spuds for their rotten dinner. So I said, 'Of course I'm not frightened of horses. I'm not frightened of anything.'

All I recall about Quilmess itself was some scrubby countryside, a couple of tatty refreshment stands, and a sort of gypsy encampment with a lot of villainous looking gypsy types and a lot of villainous looking horses.

I'd been taught to ride a horse in the bus coming along. It was simple enough; if you wanted him to go you lifted the reins off his neck, and for going left you put the rein against his neck on the right-hand side and vice versa for the other direction, and if you wanted to put the brakes on you pulled on his mouth and he stopped. Both the apprentices were apparently fairly well known to the gypsies and one of the boys could speak enough Spanish to convey to them that I was an idiot, and would they sort me out an idiot's horse?

Actually it was surprisingly comfortable sitting on the horse, once you got up there, because the saddle was very high at the back and front and covered in soft sheepskin so it felt safe and cosy and impossible to fall out of.

'Right, let's go! Vamos! Vamos!' shouted the apprentices, and disappeared with a cloud of dust and thunder of hooves into the distance.

I made no attempt to go along with them as I felt that I wasn't quite ready for the *Riders of the Purple Sage* bit just yet. I lifted the reins off the animal's neck and sure enough he walked forward and I twitched them to the right and to the left and it worked. So I steered towards the dusty track that the others had taken, and off we trotted and it was marvellous. Then the trot got a bit faster and became a canter, which suddenly became a gallop, and it was frightening. The sheepskin turned to wood and started hammering my spine and my head lolled back and forward on its string neck as the breath was thumped out of me.

We seemed to go a long way before I got enough

73

sense together to pull on the reins hard enough to stop him. Eventually he slowed, stopped, and began to eat some grass. Which in itself was another alarming experience, because suddenly there was nothing in front and it felt like the whole lot was going to slip forward over where its head used to be. Dismounting very slowly and carefully so as not to disturb it, I tied it to a bush, and sat down a safe distance away and lit a cigarette. Strangely enough I did not feel all that badly about the episode, I'd never had any desire to ride horses and it was obvious that I couldn't ride horses. Actually I felt it was a satisfying achievement to have stopped it successfully and got off. And it was a nice day and the horse was over there munching the grass and I was over here safe and sound smoking a cigarette, so all's well that ends well.

A couple of greeny brown little lizards appeared and darted in the dust about the feet of my gallant steed, attracted possibly by the cloud of insects that had turned up to suck his blood. There were some butterflies, one or two of which looked the same as those in the picture that I had bought for Green Eyes in Rio.

The cigarette finished, there was the problem of getting back. I didn't know how far I'd come and supposing I did get up on him again how could I be sure he would stop next time? I had visions of me charging back through the gypsy encampment scattering all before me, and eventually when they'd lassoed me and thrown me to the ground, I wouldn't even know the Spanish for 'I didn't do it on purpose.'

Whatever he was like to ride he was no trouble to lead. He stayed a respectful distance behind which I appreciated because I had not unnaturally developed a mistrust of him and I thought he might try and bite me. After a little while, because I was feeling a bit tired of walking and the sun was hot, I made a half-hearted attempt to get up on him, but he obviously didn't think this was a good idea and we did a few circles with him going sideways and me hopping along with one foot in the stirrup until I gave up the attempt.

When we got back I gave him to the man, had a glass of lemonade at the refreshment stand and got on a bus back to Buenos Aires and especially the Calle Viente Cinco de Mayo, the street wherein are the Splendid Bar and the Viemonte Bar and the Avalon Bar, etcetera. And where, for the price of a mug of beer and a glass of coloured water, I would find someone called Dolores or Carmencita or Maria who would listen to my tale of derring-do with wild horses on the pampas; she might not understand, but she'd listen.

That was the afternoon I found Aña Petrovitch.

Previously I'd never been in the Splendid Bar earlier than nine o'clock at night, and here it was four o'clock in the afternoon and it didn't look the same place at all.

The little bandstand was deserted and the tables were practically empty of customers. A few uniformed sailors off an Argentine battleship were drinking at one table, while at another some waiters in their white aprons and black waistcoats sat reading newspapers, and in the corner a little knot of girls scandled with shouts of shrill echoing laughter at one another.

'One beer please,' I said to the waiter.

'Media cerveza!' he shouted to the ceiling. They always shouted the order to give the bloke a chance to

75

pour it by the time they got to the bar and collected it.

' 'Ullo,' she said. ' 'Ullo Rubio ' (Rubio turns out to be Spanish for blond.)

'Hullo Aña,' I said. 'Come and sit down.' We'd been at the same table a couple of times before, when I'd been drinking with some of the firemen. But you don't always notice people so much when you're getting drunk.

She was a bit older than me, about nineteen, not very tall and a bit on the thin side. Her hair was black and her face was very lovely and very Spanish looking. Although I discovered later that her parents were actually Romanian immigrants. She took the chair opposite me.

' 'Ullo,' she said.

' 'Ullo,' I replied.

And somehow it seemed very funny, and we both laughed as if it were the funniest thing we'd heard in weeks. I don't think I'd ever laughed like that with a girl before and it was a strange, practically hysterical, sensation. Her dark eyes were shining and her face was flushed with laughter and she was becoming lovelier with every second. The waiter brought my beer and a little plate of fresh peanuts. She didn't say 'You buy me a drink' like she was supposed to do, so I said, 'Do – you – want – a – drink?' She shook her head and the waiter's face clouded over, because el Patron was not pleased with waiters who allowed girls to sit around with customers without a little glass of coloured water on the table. He sighed and shook his head reprovingly. So I ordered one just the same. And he was happy again.

When he was gone she was quiet for a few moments, then she said, 'You want to go with me?'

She somehow said the words as if she was saying, 'Are you a friend or a customer?' I still had about twelve pesos left and could easily have afforded her but for some silly reason it didn't seem right somehow.

'No,' I replied. 'No, gracias, no.'

She smiled again. 'Good,' she said. 'Good.' The waiter returned with her coloured water and I paid him.

'Cheers!'

'Saludas y pesetas!'

'What does that mean, saludas y pesetas?'

'Health and money.'

'Saludas y pesetas, Aña.'

'Saludas y pesetas, Rubio.'

She leaned across and picked some pieces of grass from my jacket, and clicked reprovingly.

'Where you been, Rubio?'

'I've been horse riding.'

She was puzzled. 'Orsridin', orsridin', what is orsridin'?'

I said, 'Well it's horse riding, isn't it?' And I did a little embarrassed mime that made her laugh and left her just as bewildered.

She shouted in Spanish to the girls at the other table and they all looked worried and said, 'Orsridin', orsridin'?' And they shouted to the waiters who shook their heads and went back to their newspapers. The guv'nor, el Patron, a fat, swarthy, sweating man in carpet slippers, came from behind the bar thumbing through a little Spanish/English dictionary and between us we found 'horse – *caballo*' and everyone shouted, 'Orsridin' – *caballo*!'

Too soon I had to go back to the ship because the

cook and his mate wouldn't have been very pleased if I'd left them to clean the galley up, especially when they discovered I hadn't been to the dentist.

Before I left she said, 'You come back tonight, Rubio?' I nearly didn't go to the Splendid Bar that evening because it all seemed a bit silly somehow, getting excited over a girl who said, 'You want to go with me?' And it wasn't as if she only said it to me, she said it to everybody. Making me feel like this is probably just one of the tricks that they play so that they'll get more money out of you than they would have done otherwise.

When I went into the Splendid that night it was all back to normal with the band blaring and everybody shouting their heads off. She was sitting at a table with some of the crew off the *Highland Princess*. She noticed me at the same time as I saw her. I didn't wave nor even nod because I felt a bit stupid. I sat down at a table in the corner by the door and toyed with the idea of going straight back to the First and Last where I'd left the bosun's peggy.

' 'Ullo, Rubio,' she said. She looked even lovelier.

'Hullo, Aña,' I said.

'*Una momenta*, I come and sit with you,' she said. 'You got some money?'

So I was right all along. I never really knew the meaning of the phrase 'My heart sank' until then, but I could actually feel it sinking inside me.

'No,' I lied.' 'I'm broke, no money, comprendo? Skint.'

She opened her hand and a crumpled peso note landed near my hand. She went away for a few minutes and I ordered a beer and some coloured water. Then she came back and sat down and said,

78

' 'Ullo.' And I said, ' 'Ullo,' and we laughed, and I gave her her peso back and my first real love affair began.

I never did go to bed with Aña Petrovitch, and we never mentioned the possibility again. Perhaps we thought of going to bed together as something a randy sailor did with a whore, and if we broke the spell that is what we might wake up as.

Every night when I could I went to the Splendid Bar for an hour or so, and nobody could make half a litre of beer and a glass of coloured water last longer than we could. Often we pored over a Spanish/English dictionary as she tried to teach me Spanish, until el Patron would catch our eye and shake his head in disapproval, and with a little goodnight kiss she would go off and sit with those who had money to spend.

Then I would walk back through the deserted docks in rapturous admiration of the lovely cranes and the beautiful warehouses and the charming rats, and say to myself, 'Isn't life wonderful?'

On Sunday I went to tea with Aña. She lived in a flat with another girl who was in the same business and worked in the First and Last. We had salad and fish for tea covered in garlic olive oil, with bread and butter, and after we'd washed up we went for a stroll and sat outside cafés drinking orange juice or coffee until it was late, then I took her home and we said goodnight like any other respectable courting couple.

We sailed for home on the Monday afternoon, and as the ship headed out into the River Plate there on the quayside in their summer dresses was a little bouquet of girls waving to us. I was too far away to see if she was there, but I think she was.

CHAPTER 4

The *Avila Star* moved slowly through the swing bridge into the King George V Dock, and on either side the people on their way home from work on that cold rainy summer evening waited in their buses and on their bikes for us to go by.

And as I leaned on the ship's rail and surveyed them loftily from above I felt as good as I ever felt in my life. I wanted one of the mortals to shout, 'Where have you come from?' so I could reply, 'Brazil and the River Plate!' But those in the buses just stared through the steamy windows and the pedestrians and cyclists hunched and stamped, impatient to be gone.

It was late when I got home. The house was clean and neat and tidy. My father said, 'Hullo boy, did you have a good trip? We didn't expect you till tomorrow, we were just off to bed.'

I gave my mother a little brooch I'd bought in Rio when I bought the picture, with a bit of the blue butterfly's wing set in glass in it. When she took it from me her hands were shaking and it was obvious that she was drying out and being very brave, you could almost hear her nerves screaming.

'I bought it in Rio,' I said. 'It's made from butterfly wing.'

She said, 'That's nice, isn't it Jerry? It'll look nice on my blue coat.' Then she said goodnight and went to bed.

When she'd gone my father whispered, 'She's had a very bad time, so for Christsake don't upset her, whatever you do.'

I said, 'What are you talking about? I'm not upsetting her. I've only just got here, haven't I?'

He sighed hopelessly. 'You haven't changed have you?' he said. 'I hoped they'd knocked some sense into you. I'm off to bed now, make yourself some cocoa if you want. Goodnight.'

When he'd gone I made a cup of cocoa and a piece of bread and dripping and sat by the fire that was nearly out. A mouse came from beneath the fireplace and I said quietly, 'Here you are mate, have a bit of bread and drippin'.' He darted away from the crumb as it landed near him and came back seconds later to snatch it and carry it away, and I thought, 'Christ, I'm sitting here like old Georgie Goodstone's mother.' And I had to laugh.

The next morning I gave my father his half pound tin of Wills' Old Friend Tobacco and my mother a couple of quid for my keep and I left the house feeling like the man who broke the bank at Monte Carlo, ready to meet old friends and regale them with stories of goings-on in faraway places that would astound and amaze them.

I stood there on the doorstep for a few moments thinking what a marvellous incredible day this was going to be, not a single spud to be peeled, no pots to wash, and nobody to say, 'Don't go to sleep boy, you're not on your daddy's yacht.'

Mrs Haynes, the lady next door, was scrubbing her step, which she did every morning come hell or highwater in sickness and in health, according to my mother, 'Just to try to show me up.'

81

'Good morning, Mrs Haynes,' I said cheerfully.

'Good morning, Dennis.' Scrub – scrub.

'It's good to be home again.'

The back of her head agreed that it was good to be home again.

'I only got home last night from Brazil and the River Plate.'

She stood up and wrung her cloth out in the bucket, and went in and closed the door. I made a mental note to boot her dog at the first opportunity.

Albert wasn't there when I got to Merino's Café, his father was there instead. I asked for a glass of lemonade and a piece of cake with pink icing. When he'd served me I said, 'Where's Albert?'

'He'sa nod'ere,' he grunted in his usual charming old Italian manner. I didn't have the nerve to ask where Maria was in case he pulled a knife on me. As he counted my change on the counter he said, 'You ina 'ere Saturday night?'

I said, 'No, I was coming up the English Channel on my way back from Brazil.' His brown eyes fixed me from his little brown face.

'Themalayabouts breaka sixa glasses, you know about that?'

I said, 'Of course I do, it was on the wireless, a special broadcast to ships at sea.' He didn't get upset because he'd only been over here for about thirty years and if you spoke more than three words at a time he didn't know what you were talking about.

Georgie Waghorn and Tommy Davies came in just then.

'Hullo Blondie,' they said.

I said, 'Hullo Georgie, hullo Tom, am I glad to see

82

you, I thought I was going to spend the rest of the day talking to old bloody monkey face here.'

Georgie said, 'Did you get that letter about the bird in the Red Lion you were after?'

I said, 'Yes, I got it in Rio. Now there's a place you'd like, have a cup of tea or something. I'll tell you a few things that will make your hair curl.'

Tommy said, 'Look, we can't stop now, we're going down the gasworks to see about a couple of jobs. We've only come in for some fags.' They put a penny each and bought five Woodbines between them and left.

'See you tonight,' they said.

I waited a little while to see if Albert or Maria would turn up, and then I went in and had a chat with Joe the greengrocer. He was pleased to see me but customers kept coming in so I said I'd see him sometime.

Then I wandered round to Bert Tracey's house just for something to do and to find out his whereabouts in the world at this time. I was really overjoyed when his mother told me that he was at home. Although he wasn't there at the moment because he'd been out of work almost since I sailed on the *Avila Star*, and he'd gone over the docks as usual to try to get a ship. So I said I'd go and have a drink in the Red Lion, and if he came home soon that's where I'd be. I don't know why I chose the Red Lion, I suppose for the same reason some people stick needles in themselves and whip one another with scented bootlaces.

By the time Bert walked in I was on my fourth pint and really wallowing in a cosy morass of self pity about my lost love, the beautiful green-eyed goddess who used to rest her incredibly lovely elbows on the very bar that I was leaning on.

83

Bert was a bit shabbier than of yore but just as jaunty and full of himself as ever. I was so pleased to see him, I ordered him a pint and a double whisky before he'd hardly got to the bar.

'I knew you was home,' he said. 'I saw the *Avila* in the KG Five. And, wait for it, I've got a ship for both of us, a little tramp boat lying at Ranks Mills over at Millwall sailing next week. How about that?'

I said, 'Ease off, I only came ashore last night. I'm going to have a little holiday before I go back again. I've just done three and a half months without a day off.'

He shook his head and sighed, 'If you'll give me a chance to tell you,' he said. 'What I'm trying to say is that this is practically a holiday ship. There's only twenty-eight in the crew, a nice friendly crowd, been with her for years. There's no bullshit on those tramps, and if there was, she is so small we could scrub the ship out in half an hour, if we had to, which we won't.'

I said, 'Anyway I'm going back in the *Avila Star*, so have another pint and shut up about your tramp boat while I tell you about this girl I met in Buenos Aires.'

He said, 'You'll have a long wait for the *Avila*, she's going round to Tyneside for a refit or something.'

'How do you know that?'

'I met a couple of the sailors in the Shipping Federation this morning who are taking her round there.'

At that time I didn't know Bert Tracey intimately enough to know that he could be one of the most accomplished liars you've ever met, so we sang 'Buddy can you spare a dime' and signed on the MV *Innismoor* the following afternoon.

The *Innismoor* turned out to be all that Bert had

84

claimed of her, she was small and she was dirty. And the first of many shocks aboard what was to be our home for the next eight months came when the steward, a crafty little Welshman with an enormous hooked nose whom Bert immediately nicknamed the Cherrypicker because 'he could hang on with his nose and pick with both hands,' showed us to our quarters, a little two-berth cabin situated up on the after poop-deck between the two lifeboats.

'One of you will have to get himself a donkey's breakfast,' he said.

'What's a bleedin' donkey's breakfast?' enquired Bert.

The Cherrypicker seemed surprised. 'A palliasse of straw for your bunk,' he said. 'One of these.' He shook up a dirty mattress which occupied the bottom bunk.

'Someone's nicked the other one.'

'Well I'll claim that one,' said Bert. 'Where's our blankets?'

'The Company doesn't supply any bedding,' said the Cherrypicker.

Neither of us had ever been on a ship that didn't supply sheets and blankets but there was no going back now, and arguing wouldn't change anything.

'We'll soon sort out a couple of blankets,' said Bert cheerfully. 'Where we bound for, Steward?'

'Archangel to load pit-props for the mines in South Africa,' replied the Cherrypicker.

'Where's Archangel?'

'Russia, up north in the White Sea.'

'Christ almighty,' I said, 'we'll freeze to death!'

'No you won't, sonny, it's summer time up there now, the sun shines all day and all night.'

The night we joined her, three days later, my

85

mother had gone back on the booze and the house was empty, so I took a parcel of blankets that the tullyman had left on approval, also the corduroy cushion seats off the fireside chairs, and I had a bunk aboard the *Innismoor* that was the envy of all who viewed it. Although I don't suppose that my parents were too pleased when they rolled home that night and found themselves about a fiver in debt and nothing to sit on.

Ten days we were in Archangel. Ten days and the only women we ever saw were very solid looking ladies digging the roads or working on the timber in the docks. Before we left I'd learned enough Russian to get a smile out of them.

'Dobre, dobre!' I'd cry, 'Niet panimayo!' I never really expected 'Very good, I don't understand,' however beautifully pronounced, to inflame the passions of a Russian maiden to throw aside her pick and shovel and rush me home for a quick cuppa out of the samovar and a roll on the wolf-skins, but it was worth a try and a smile was better than nothing.

Bert Tracey had a theory that sex was probably illegal in that part of the world, a theory not completely without substance because nearly everything else was. It was illegal to smoke in the streets, illegal for us to possess Russian money, illegal to possess a camera, illegal to go anywhere without a pass, illegal to get drunk. So it is not out of the bounds of possibility that screwing was illegal as well.

I'd had a foreboding about Russia ever since the Cherrypicker broke the news that that was where we were going, although in truth I knew very little about the place. Up to then my knowledge of Russia was drawn from a lovely dramatic picture that hung in my Auntie Lilly's front room depicting a horse-drawn sledge full of men in furry hats rushing at breakneck speed across the snow hotly pursued by a pack of wolves. It was called *In Peril on the Steppes*. I also remember my mother denouncing the Russian Bolsheviks who were shooting everybody in their own country and when they were finished they'd be coming over to do the same to us. So my idea of Russia was roughly that of a very cold place where if the local wildlife didn't get you the Bolsheviks would.

So when the *Innismoor* had been stopped on arrival just outside Archangel and boarded by a boat-load of ragged, fully armed soldiers of the Red Army I can perhaps be forgiven my remark to Bert Tracey: 'You stupid bastard, you've got us captured.'

But as luck would have it they didn't want to capture us. All they required was that we should line up around the ship's rail and be eaten alive by clouds of the most vicious mosquitoes in the world for two hours while they searched in the ship for arms and cameras and binoculars, and removed the rockets and provisions from the lifeboats. Then, when they were satisfied that a plot by twenty-eight undernourished British seamen to take over their country had been nipped in the bud, they relaxed and sat on the hatches and rolled fat cigarettes in pieces of newspaper and grinned and pointed at us and said, 'Dobre! Dobre!' But if the welcome to Mother Russia left anything to be desired we still had the farewell to savour.

He appeared in the doorway of the galley on the morning of our last day in port. I was having a mug of tea and a chat with Bert and the cook. We didn't think he was one of the natives because he didn't look like any Russians we'd seen up to then; he was wearing a nice, well-cut, light coloured sports coat and flannels and he was smiling, whereas the other civilians we'd seen were mostly drab and miserable looking. And when he spoke he spoke with an American accent.

He put one foot on the breakwater and leaned in the galley doorway.

'Hullo there, Cooky!' he shouted. 'How's she going? Hullo boys, good to meet you!'

We nodded. 'This is your last day isn't it?' he continued. 'So you're away tomorrow?'

The cook said, 'Yes, thank Christ. The sooner we're out of this stinking rotten dump the better.'

He said, 'My name is Alex, I'm with the port authorities.' And he shook us each warmly by the hand. The cook went pale.

'I thought you were a Yank,' he said. 'I didn't mean . . .'

The man cut him short. 'Don't worry, don't worry,' he said. 'Between you and me this is a sonofabitch town to be in. Now Moscow, that's the place. D'you ever go to Moscow?'

'No, I've not had that pleasure,' shouted the cook hysterically, 'but I've heard it's very nice.'

Bert and I smiled at each other, the poor bastard was really frightened. A soldier had shot one of the sailors off a Swedish boat last week because he was too drunk to stop walking and get his pass out of his pocket, and now the cook was afraid it was going to happen to him.

'I'm telling you you'd love Moscow, that is some city. And one day, when the workers of the world have destroyed the capitalists and thrown off their shackles, we'll all meet in Moscow, won't we comrades?'

He was beginning to sound like one of the speakers

from the Greenwich Communist Party who got chased up and down Nelson Street on Saturday nights by the mounted police. He must have seen by our expressions that he was losing us.

'But there I go,' he was smiling again, 'I mustn't forget what I've come aboard for. I want you all to be my guests tonight. A little place on the other side of town, just a few guys off some of the boats, we'll sit around, maybe see a film, chew the fat, drink a few bottles of beer. What d'you say?'

Bert said, 'Is the beer free?' Alex looked hurt.

'What do you think of this guy?' he asked us. 'Is the beer free? You got any roubles?' We shook our heads vigorously. You could be put in prison for having roubles.

'Then it's got to be free, hasn't it comrades? Eight o'clock then? Don't worry about getting there, I'll have some trucks here on the quay to pick you up. We'll have one hell of a night. Now I'm just going to have a word with the guys in the fo'c'sle. See you tonight, comrades.' A warm handshake and he was gone.

When we got off the truck that night in company with most of the fo'c'sle crowd we were ushered into a sort of village hall with rows of wooden benches and a platform at the far end. The place was about half full of seamen, perhaps two hundred, of various nationalities, mostly British, Swedes, Danes and Norwegians.

When we sat down and the doors were closed, four or five men, our friend Alex among them, appeared on the platform and took their seats at the table. Then one of them came forward and started talking. He said, 'Good evening, comrades, we all know why we're

89

here tonight. You have come to learn how you too can find freedom and loose the yoke and shackles of your masters the imperialists.'

Dell whispered, 'I didn't come to learn anything, I came for the piss up.'

I said, 'I suppose it's like the Seamen's Mission, you have to listen to the sermon before you get the tea and cakes.'

Speaker followed speaker, and phrases and names were constantly repeated . . . workers of the world . . . chains and shackles . . . Marx and Lenin . . . capitalist imperialist . . . revolutionary councils. And to make it even more boring, after each speaker one of the other men on the platform would step forward and interpret what the last man had said.

Alex was the last to speak. He told us of his good work organizing the trade union movement in America. He also mentioned Henry Ford's private army whose function it was to deal with would-be trade unionists. And it wasn't until many years later, when I read Upton Sinclair's *The Flivver King*, that I realized he might have been speaking the truth. Then suddenly they were singing the *Internationale* and the doors were opened and it was all over. We wandered out into the everlasting sunshine and looked around for Alex to tell us where the beer was, but he had disappeared.

Our truck was still there, and we said to the driver, 'Where's this free beer?' and made signs like drinking a bottle of beer. He grinned and pointed to the truck, and when we were all aboard it he drove straight back to the ship. And that night as far as the crew of the MV *Innismoor* were concerned, the cause of International Communism had received a blow from which it would never recover, and could go and get stuffed.

The *Innismoor* was what was known among seamen as a hungry ship, and the further she got from land the hungrier we became. And because she had no refrigerators any fresh meat or vegetables had to be served up as quickly as possible before they went bad, and in some cases just after they'd gone bad.

Our first inkling of just how hungry we were going to be had manifested itself the day we left London, when I went to get some stores for myself and the engineers from the Cherrypicker in his storeroom. It was all right until he came to the condensed milk.

'Eight engineers,' he said, 'that's eight tins of milk and one for yourself, and don't come back before your three weeks are up.'

I said, 'What's three weeks got to do with it?'

He said, 'It's simple enough, sonny, one tin one man three weeks, that's the ration.'

I said, 'One man one tin three weeks! What's this supposed to be, a ship or an effing lifeboat?'

He took my arm in his claw and led me over to a printed sheet pinned to the bulkhead.

'Can you read, boy? Then read that.'

The notice was headed, 'Scale of Weekly Provisions. Merchant Navy Shipping Act 1906.' And there down the list of goodies . . . 'salt pork 3lbs . . . soft bread and ship's biscuits 7lbs . . .' was 'milk condensed ⅓lb'.

He said, 'OK. You've seen it, Board of Trade Rations in black and white, one 1lb tin of milk one man three weeks. If you've got any arguments go up and have a chat with the Old Man, he's dying for a bit of company.'

A couple of weeks later when we were leaving

Archangel, I went along for the stores and I said to him, 'No wonder we didn't see you at the meeting about overthrowing this lot that is starving the workers, you're one of the bastards that's doing it.' But he only laughed.

But apart from the grub, life was pretty good on the *Innismoor*. The captain never inspected the ship nor made a nuisance of himself, preferring to stay up on the bridgedeck with his box of carpenter's tools making reproduction antique furniture. In fact we never even had a lifeboat drill until one of the sailors fell overboard outside Durban and it took about five minutes to lower the lifeboat.

All I had to do every day was collect the grub at mealtimes and put it on the table for the engineers and their apprentices, and wash up a few plates, have a sweep round and a scrub out, clean the chief engineer's cabin, and that was it.

There was quite a bit of brass work around like there is on all ships but I didn't clean it because the bosun kept all his Bluebell for the brass work on the bridge, and the chief engineer wouldn't give me any more after I conveniently lost the few tins he did part with. Once, when he thought the brass was getting a bit too green, the second engineer showed me his discovery of how to clean it with Rose's Lime Juice, so I reported him to the steward who gave him a rollicking because the Lime Juice was issued to stop us getting scurvy or jumping on one another, not to clean the brass with.

When we were about a month out of Archangel the spuds that were left in the spud-locker went too mouldy to do anything with and, much to Bert the galley boy's delight, we had to throw them over the

92

side. After that it was rice with everything, and eventually weevils with everything. At first I couldn't eat weevils but by now they were in the porridge and the flour and everything that wasn't in a tin. So, because there were too many of them to keep fishing out, I used to sprinkle tea leaves on my food so that I couldn't see which were weevils and which were tea leaves. But after a while I got fed up with having tea leaves all over my dinner and I ate my weevils like everybody else.

Before we got to Durban the meals were getting really bad. The only one who didn't complain was the chief engineer, a big fat man from Huddersfield. He used to preside at the head of the table like Captain Blyth himself. And when someone passed a remark about the everlasting salt port or tinned rabbit he'd say things like, 'Come now Mr Jarvis, I'm sure the cook is doing his best, we've been at sea a long time and these things will happen y'know.'

Actually he was entitled to be a bit cheerful because not only were he and the captain shareholders in the Company but they both had big private stores of tinned food in their cabins which they ate when no one was looking. I first discovered his cache, in a cupboard, when I was cleaning one day. I said, 'Blimey, that's a nice lot of grub, Chief.'

And he said, 'That, my boy, is part of the ship's emergency rations, and if I ever find you've laid one finger on one tin of it I'll kick your arse from here to Shanghai!'

It took us forty-five days to get to Durban, and by the thirtieth day even the weevils had gone off some of the stuff we were eating, but I still didn't see the chief engineer dishing out any of the 'ship's emergency rations'. Not to us, anyway.

And by about day thirty-five the bosun put a padlock on the fresh water pump outside the galley so that people couldn't use it for washing in. But as the fresh water had long since taken on the colour and consistency of cocoa there wasn't much point in washing in it anyway, unless you wanted to look like a Christy Minstrel. For cooking and drinking you either had to let it settle overnight or take a bucket down to the engine room and get some from the condensers.

But of course the voyage had its lighter moments, and if you could forget your last meal and try not to think about the next one it wasn't too bad.

One of the lighter moments was when Bert got a bit too saucy with the Cherrypicker, who promptly gave him a tin of soft soap and told him to take up the long coconut fibre runners from the alleyway of the officers' cabins and scrub them on deck with a broom.

Now it so happens that on the *Avila Star* I had seen coconut runners tied to a rope and trailed over the stern, where an hour surfing in the ship's wake had cleaned them marvellously. So in no time at all Bert had obtained a long heaving line from somewhere and we tied all the runners securely together, fastened one end of the line to the rail and between us heaved the mats over the stern. They hit the water and drifted away in the ship's wake until they became a dot like a patch of seaweed and disappeared for ever in the vastness of the Indian Ocean; the line had broken about twenty feet from where it was made fast to the rail. We both realized what had happened as soon as the runners were a hundred yards away on a forty-foot line.

I looked at Bert and his eyes were staring, his mouth

94

had come open and he was making strange noises. I think he was trying to say, 'Come back! Come back!' But he had lost the power of speech. He grabbed the line and pulled it frantically hand over hand inboard, and stood looking at the broken end as if he expected the runners to reappear on it.

'It's broken,' he said at last. I said, 'I can see that.' And I started laughing until I couldn't stand up for laughing.

'You bastard!' he shouted, 'you knew this would happen.' I looked up at him and tried to say, 'I'm sorry, but I didn't know the line would break.' But it wouldn't come, and all I could do was shake my head.

His anger subsided into self-pity. 'He'll make me pay for them,' he said bitterly, 'he'll say I did it on purpose, that's what he'll say. I'll have to tell him.' By a great effort of will-power I stopped laughing and, standing up, put my hand reassuringly on his shoulder where he now leant over the rail staring into the ship's wake.

'Of course he can't make you pay,' I said. 'For Christsake it was an accident, accidents will happen.'

'I'll go and tell him,' he muttered. 'Get it over with.' And he walked away.

A couple of minutes later I could hear raised voices. Bert was plaintive. 'I'm sorry Chief, but it was an accident.' And the Cherrypicker was saying, 'I wouldn't put it past you to chuck them over the side just to drop me in it with the Old Man.' They appeared round the corner of the deckhouse, and Bert said, 'Well here's the bit of line I had them tied to, d'you believe me now?'

But I'd already untied the line and it had followed the runners. Bert said, 'Where's the line gone,

95

Blondie?' I said, 'What line?' And for a moment he stared in speechless disbelief at this awful thing his friend had done to him.

'You rotten sod,' he said, and then he couldn't stop himself laughing and neither could I. And the little Cherrypicker looked from one to the other in total bewilderment and snarled, 'I'll report this to the captain, maybe that'll take the smile off your faces, when you have to pay for 'em.' But we never did.

When we got to Africa it was raining. A cold grey morning that really belonged more to winter in Bethnal Green than Africa. Although after that ridiculous sunshine arrangement in Russia I wasn't really altogether surprised.

When we came alongside and tied up, a long row of squatting men started slowly rising to their feet from where they were crouching out of the rain against the wall of the warehouses. They were black and ragged, some held old sacks over their shoulders, some had nothing, and others tattered umbrellas.

Three white men appeared from somewhere and started shouting at them in a foreign language and they moved over to where the gangway was coming down. A couple that were slow in rising were kicked by one of the white men, and I thought there was going to be a bit of a punch-up, but they didn't even look at the man that kicked them and just jogged over to join their mates at the foot of the gangway. These were the stevedores.

A bit later in the day when the sun was shining it began to seem a bit more like Africa because you could stand on the fo'c'sle head and see stretches of greenery that might be the legendary African jungle about a mile past the conglomeration of ships and

The 'Innismoor'. She couldn't have been too bad—
fifty million weevils can't be wrong.

machinery. I said to one of the white men, 'Where's the lions?'

He said, 'What lions?'

I said, 'The lions and buffaloes and things, this is Africa isn't it?'

'Oh,' he said, 'you're talking about big game. You'd want to be about three or four days up country from here, maybe more than that even.'

Another illusion gone for a Burton. I would have liked to have seen some wild lions. I didn't even ask him if it was four days on a bus or a train or walking, it was certain I wasn't going to get four days off, and even if I did I wasn't going to manage it with the two pounds sub that was all the skipper would let us have because he was still fretting about his rotten mats.

I said, 'Why d'you keep kicking these fellers?' He didn't seem to know what I meant at first.

'Fellers? Oh, the kaffirs! It's good for 'em, they're used to it.'

I said, 'Aren't you worried they'll stick a spear in you one day?'

He laughed and said, 'They won't do that so long as I keep kicking 'em.'

Later on I said to him, 'Where do you go for girls around here?'

'What sort of girls . . . whores?'

'Yes.'

'How much money you got?'

'Not much.'

He peered down into the hold where the stevedores were unloading the pit-props we'd brought from Archangel, shouted something at one of the men who was sitting down and threw a lump of wood at him.

'What you want to do is to go up town and get a

rickshaw boy to take you up to the Old Dutch Road,'
he said. 'Don't pay him more than half what he asks
for and if he gets saucy give him a smack in the
mouth.'

By about eight o'clock that evening we'd had a few
beers and were heading for the Old Dutch Road in fine
style, in a smart rickshaw with big wheels, pulled
effortlessly at a trot by a massive half naked Zulu with
ostrich plumes nodding on his head-dress. As soon as
Bert told him we wanted to go up to the Old Dutch
Road he knew what it was all about.

'You want some girls, boss?' he said. 'You leave it to
me, I get you lovely girls. OK boss?'

'OK Rastus,' said Bert. 'We'll leave it to you, off we
go then.'

It was a nice feeling sitting up there just bowling
along and watching the world go by.

'Who's going to give him that smack in the mouth
you were telling me about?' asked Bert, indicating
our Zulu with a nod of his head. I looked at those
massive black shoulders, muscles rippling with every
movement of the shafts, and shuddered at the very
thought of what their owner could do to you if the
mood took him.

'Keep your voice down, you bloody fool,' I whispered. 'If he gets upset he could kill the pair of us with
one hand behind his back.'

'And eat us,' said Bert, 'although I bet old Rastus
there wouldn't eat us if he knew some of the crap
we've been feeding on for the last couple of months.'

The door was opened by a very large black lady.
Our Zulu said something to her in their own language
and her expression changed from one of slight bel-
ligerence to a flashing welcoming smile.

'Come right in, gentlemen,' she said.

'Rastus, wait here for us, we won't be long, OK?'

'OK boss, I wait here.' He took a clay pipe from the leopard skin at his waist and sat on his heels between the shafts.

The room she ushered us into was dingy with a stone floor, and lit by a smoking oil lamp on the wall. The furniture consisted of a small wooden table and some chairs in the centre of the room, and against the far wall a settee on which an old man was resting. The woman shouted something to him and he sat up and blinked blearily at us. She apparently wanted him to leave but instead he took a swig from a bottle beside him on the floor and settled down again. She spat at him and returned to us.

'Now if you two gentlemen would like to make yourselves comfortable,' she said, indicating the rickety chairs round the dirty table, 'I'll go and find you two nice young ladies and we'll all have a bottle of wine together.'

'Yes, thank you,' said Bert. 'That'll be very nice, won't it, Blondie?'

'Yes,' I replied without too much enthusiasm, because something about this place was making me nervous. 'Yes, that'll be very nice.'

'Now who is going to give me five shillings for the wine?' she asked, thrusting a big dusky palm under our noses. I gave her five shillings and she went off somewhere out the front door.

We sat and looked at each other, and the old man stirred, then sat up, took a swig from his bottle and silently proffered it to us. We shook our heads and I said, 'No thank you, we'll wait till the lady gets back.'

The lady returned almost immediately, in her hand a quart bottle with no label on it, and followed somewhat reluctantly by two raggedly dressed black girls in their ourly teens.

'There you are gentlemen,' she announced triumphantly. 'Two beautiful girls, Sonia and Gladys, and a nice bottle of the best of the grape.'

She found two tin mugs and a cup and pulled the cork from the bottle with a set of teeth in a mouth big enough to take the head off a shark, then poured a drop in each receptacle. Bert was the first to take a mouthful.

'Christ almighty,' he choked. 'What's this, bloody petrol?'

Our hostess opened her sharktrap and laughed loud and long. 'That's very funny sir,' she gasped. 'No, this is not petrol sir, this is what I told you, the best of the grape.' Her voice lowered to a whisper, 'We make it ourselves from a secret recipe.' Actually it wasn't too bad after the first mouthful. It did taste a bit like petrol, probably because it had been matured in a petrol can.

Sonia and Gladys stood silent, and rolled the whites of their eyes at us. The lady made some small conversation about how nice it was to have such fine company, told us her name was Sarah and topped our mugs up. It was a pretty potent brew.

'Are they the best you can find?' asked Bert, tipping his chair back and nodding towards the girls.

She beckoned us forward. 'They're virgins,' she whispered. 'A pound each, two pounds OK?' She held out her hand.

Bert was beginning to feel the 'best of the grape'.

'Piss off,' he said scornfully, 'I wouldn't give you a

pound for the both of 'em, anyway I don't fancy 'em, do you Blondie?'

I shook my head, 'Not for me thank you.'

She leaned forward again. 'Well,' she whispered, 'how about the three of us, those two and me for two pounds?' I started laughing, and Bert pointed his thumb at the old man dozing on the settee behind him.

'What about old Uncle Tom here, don't he do a turn?' he asked. While we were enjoying the joke she said something to the girls and they left as silently as they'd arrived. Then she topped us up again and joined in the laughter and I suddenly noticed that the old man had gone as well. I said, 'I think we'd better be going then.'

Bert said, 'All right, let's finish the bottle, then we'll be off.'

I said, 'Old grandad has disappeared, I think we could be in a bit of trouble here, you please yourself, I'm off in case he comes back with reinforcements.'

Bert's expression suddenly went very sober. 'Blimey, you could be right Blondie, let's get out of here!'

We both staggered a bit as we got up from the table. Our hostess who hadn't looked very pretty previously was now looking decidedly ugly.

'You got to give me ten shillings hospitality money,' she said. Bert took the bottle off the table by the neck and made as if to swing at her with it. I caught his arm before it went any further. I was sober enough not to chance being in the second round of a punch-up with somebody's mammy when the family called.

'We'll come back tomorrow,' I said. 'We'll bring some more money, you get some better girls for us, OK?'

She said, 'You won't come back.'

I said, 'An Englishman's word, missus, an Englishman's word is his bond, right?' It was a choice between believing an Englishman's word was his bond or the chance of a clout with more than half a bottle of the 'best of the grape'.

'OK, see you tomorrow night, sir, get some special girls, now don't you forget, eh?'

The rickshaw was still outside the door. There was no sign of the cavalry, and we woke Rastus up and got in. I said, 'OK Rastus, back to the docks, let's go.'

Bert still had the bottle and we both took a swig as the Zulu picked up the shafts. Sarah was standing in the doorway, 'Don't forget sir, tomorrow night!' Bert leaned over the back of the rickshaw and blew her a Bronx cheer, which he was very good at.

I said, 'Take it easy, old Rastus here might be a relative of hers.'

Bert looked at me with bleary eyes. 'What, old Rastus? Of course he's not, he's a Zulu, a loyal friend of the white man, our mate.'

I said, 'It's the Gurkhas who are the true friends of the white man. It was this lot that slaughtered us all at Rorke's Drift, I remember reading about it in the Rover or it might have been the Wizard.'

'Leave off,' he said scornfully. 'You don't believe everything you read in your comics do you? Rastus! Ain't your lot true friends of the white man!?' The black man's head half turned towards us with a flash of white teeth and nodding plumes, 'Yes boss!'

I knew he was wrong but not wishing to open old scores I said, 'Let's give Rastus a drink, pull up Rastus, have a drop of the best of the grape!' He stopped and, putting the shafts on the ground, took the proffered bottle and drained it in one gulp, grinned and tossed the empty bottle into some bushes by the roadside and picked up the shafts again.

Bert said, 'Look at the greedy bastard, you're right Blondie, he's no friend of the white man, he's drunk all our best of the grape.'

By the time we were getting near the ship the Zulu was beginning to feel the effects of the wine as well. We were singing 'Buddy can you spare a dime' and 'A shanty in old Shanty Town' and he was leaping about like a two year old. I had an idea. I said, 'Next time he jumps up in the air let's both sit on the hood and keep him up there, I'll tell you when . . . now!'

We both sat on the folds of the collapsible hood behind us and Rastus stayed up there, bare feet flaying the empty air, until one of the wheels hit a cart-rut or something and the whole lot slewed to the side of the road and turned over in the ditch. We picked ourselves up, there was no sign of the Zulu, he must have catapulted off into the undergrowth.

The wheels of the rickshaw were still turning slowly in the moonlight. I said, 'Blimey, we've done it now, what shall we do?' Bert was holding his elbow and making moaning sounds and suddenly without answering he broke into a staggering run down the road in the direction we'd been going, and not wishing to be left alone with Rastus, dead or alive, I followed him.

The next morning one of the engineers said to me, 'I see your mate has got a bad arm and you look a bit rough, what did you two get up to last night?'

I said, 'Nothing much, we had a ride in a rickshaw and he fell out.' I didn't want to say too much because what with poor old Rastus and those two little black girls I was feeling a bit ashamed of the whole episode.

CHAPTER 5

We left Africa in the cold grey dawn, just as we had arrived. The *Innismoor*, loaded now with coal for Sebang, a bunkering station off Sumatra on the other side of the Indian Ocean, heaved out of the harbour and met the ocean with creaks and groans as if she relished the journey even less than we did.

I was disappointed in Africa. Just as Russia had been nothing like the picture in my Auntie Lilly's, so the Africa that I'd seen bore no resemblance to the talking pictures, *Africa Speaks* or *Cape to Cairo*, at the New Cross Cinema, all seats sixpence in the afternoon, two features, a Newsreel and Fred Slunge at the mighty Wurlitzer.

No lions had roared for me, no leopards had leapt . . . no sign of Thomson's gazelle . . . nor for that matter Thomson himself. No rhino had wheeled into a thundering charge. Not that I wanted to be charged by a thundering rhinoceros but I wouldn't have minded watching it happen to somebody else.

Sebang, when we got there a month later, turned out to be an island with nothing much to offer except a palm-fringed lagoon, a jetty for unloading the coal, and a trading post run by a Chinaman who sold everything from a packet of fags to a new anchor chain. The rest was coconut plantation and jungle.

When we'd cleared up after the midday meal we

went up and asked the skipper if we could have a sub out of our wages.

'No, you can't have any money,' he said, with that easy camaraderie that one finds betwixt captains and galley boys. 'If I give you money you'll go ashore and get drunk with it. What you both need is some working gear. Look at you, you look like a pair of bloody beachcombers, you're a disgrace to my ship.'

True, we had been wearing the same trousers and singlets for nearly four months and the uppers had long since parted with the soles of our shoes, but how we could be a disgrace to a ship that, it was rumoured, was only kept together by the rust and the cockroaches holding hands was hard to imagine.

He thought for a moment. 'I'll tell you what I'll do,' he said, 'I'll give you a chit for three pounds between you to buy some working clothes, wait there.'

He disappeared into his cabin and returned within a couple of minutes bearing a piece of note paper with the 'Runciman Line' heading and some writing on it.

'Here,' he said, 'Take this up to the store and give it to the Chinaman, and if you try to buy anything but clothes with it I'll have you both with a paint brush in your hand till ten o'clock every night from here to Saigon, you see if I don't, off you go now.'

The bosun was leaning on the rail by the gangway as we went ashore. I said, 'Here Bos', where's Saigon?'

He said, 'It's a fair way from here, laddie, French Indo-China.'

Bert said, 'I thought we were going home.'

'Aye, one day laddie, one day.'

Bert was even more downcast than I was at the prospect of no girls, no booze and now Indo-China, wherever that might be.

As we mooched along the jetty to the store, I stopped to look at the coral fish and a turtle about as big as a dustbin lid came right underneath me, I said, 'Look Bert, a turtle!'

He said, 'Sod the turtle.' And kept on walking. A few minutes later, by the side of the path, I noticed a bush comprised almost entirely of stick insects but he didn't want to look at that either.

The trading post was a long shed built on stilts with a veranda on which were a couple of tables and a few chairs. The Chinaman, dressed in dirty tropical whites and a pith helmet, was asleep in one of the chairs and he woke up and said, 'Hullo please,' took our chit and ushered us inside the store, a veritable Aladdin's cave of everything, clothing, boxes of cigars, lighters, rifles, revolvers, animal skins and cartons of cigarettes with names nobody had ever heard of, it was all there. We selected some white cotton trousers, shirts and singlets and a couple of pairs of canvas shoes each.

Bert said, 'You got any beer?'

The Chinaman said, 'No beer for this,' indicating the captain's chitty, 'You like beer, something more, you sign more chitties, OK? You pay tomorrow, OK?'

Bert's face lit up, 'OK Johnny, four beers pay tomorrow, OK?'

The Chinaman went off to get the beer and we sat down at one of the tables on the veranda.

'How're we going to pay this feller tomorrow?' I asked.

Bert said, 'I dunno, that's his worry, ain't it? I'm going to get pissed before he changes his mind, that's all I know.'

When the Chinaman came back with four bottles

and a couple of glasses, Bert took the chit and the pencil off him and wrote on it, then he passed it to me saying, 'Here Blondie, you've got to sign as well, you can't keep poncin' on me all your life.' I took the chit and noticed that Bert Tracey was now Dean Swift Esq. So I signed Lloyd George and gave it back to the man, who grinned cheerfully and went back into the store.

When we'd finished the beer we went inside and bought a few cartons of cigarettes called Four Aces that were almost half as cheap as the shilling per fifty Player's Medium and Wills Goldflake aboard the ship. We also signed for some lighters and penknives because, you never knew, there might be some whores in Saigon who were in need of lighters and penknives. We were the only customers so the Chinaman must have thought it was a lucky day when Dean Swift and Lloyd George turned up.

'You like drop of gin?' he asked. And taking a bottle off the shelf poured two tots of colourless liquid which tasted not unike the 'best of the grape' and was probably the Sumatran version of the same. I never was a spirit drinker so I gave mine to Bert who seemed to have taken a liking to the stuff.

We sat about another hour on the veranda. I had a few more beers and Bert a few more gins. We'd sung 'Stormy weather', 'Underneath the arches' and were well into 'Hallelujah I'm a bum' when the steward turned up with a couple of the deck officers and sat at the next table. They'd only been there a couple of minutes when the steward said, 'Can you lads keep it down a bit? We can hardly hear ourselves speak over here.'

We stopped in full flight, 'Hallelujah I'm a bum . . . Hallelujah bum again . . . Hallelujah give us a handout to . . .' and I said, 'What d'you say, Chiefy? I couldn't hear you for all the noise this feller's making.'

He said, 'I told you to keep it down a bit, we can't hear ourselves speak.'

Bert was well under the influence of the firewater. He looked blearily at the steward and said, 'Well get up a tree, you cherrypickin' bastard.' He staggered to his feet, tipping the table so that the bottles and glasses crashed to the floor. 'And what's more if you don't like it you can come outside.' The fact that we were outside seemed to have escaped him. He sat down again with a bump.

Suddenly the Chinaman was looming over us, he was a big Chinaman. 'You go now, you come back tomorrow, OK?'

He pushed our parcels at us, and Bert pushed them back again. The second mate at the other table said, 'I should do as the man says boys, these people can get very nasty if you're not careful.'

'Come on Bert,' I said. 'Let's get out of here.'

We took our parcels and staggered down the steps of the veranda and off down the path to the beach.

'Underneath the arches,' I shouted, 'I'll dream my dreams away . . .'

'Why don't you shut up?' snarled Bert. 'You and your big mouth are always getting me in trouble.'

An excess of spirits always made Bert a bit unreliable, and a gutful of local firewater after a month or five weeks' abstinence was apparently not going to make him the nicest person to be with in the near future.

'I could have sorted that Chink out if you hadn't been so frightened,' he maudled.

108

'Well anyway,' I replied, 'well anyway, well anyway, I'm not frightened of you mate, so don't push your bloody luck, just don't push your bloody luck that's all.' I do tend to repeat myself when I'm drunk.

He dropped his parcels and turned facing me, then changed his mind and started to relieve himself against a palm ree. Suddenly his eyes focused blearily somewhere behind me and he shouted, 'Christ, they're after us!' and still relieving himself ran crashing off into the jungle.

I stood for a moment, as they say, nonplussed by the turn of events. Whatever had sent my friend galloping off into the unknown was probably a figment of his feverish imagination, but whatever it was I wasn't so drunk as to follow him into somewhere that was said to be riddled with poisonous snakes, spiders, and even, so they said, the terrible orang-utans.

With difficulty I began to gather up his abandoned parcels and as I did so they were upon me. Six natives, bare-chested, barefoot, dressed like the others I'd seen in short ragged trousers or white skirts, some carrying long knives at the waist. They were laughing and chattering quietly as they came.

'Hullo,' I drooled ingratiatingly. 'Just been doing a bit of shopping, my mate has gone for a slash,' indicating the green hell behind me. They padded past with hardly a glance and disappeared down the track.

When I got down to the edge of the jungle near the beach I saw Bert staggering along in the distance. He fell over a couple of times. And when I got near I shouted, 'Oi, Tracey! Come and carry your gear, I'm not your bloody servant!' When he stopped and turned I could see that he was covered in scratches from his trip into the undergrowth and his eyes were

sort of glazed and wild looking. That so-called gin
was really taking a toll of him.

'Come on mate,' I said, 'Let's sit down and have a
smoke, it's all right, they've gone now.' I dropped the
parcels and sat down on the ground. He lurched
towards me then suddenly stopped and shouted, 'No
they haven't, the bastards are in there!' And threw
himself punching and kicking into a large bush, the
bush where I'd seen the stick insects. I jumped up and
tried to pull him away and he turned on me and
punched me in the mouth. I managed to hit him a
couple of times and he suddenly collapsed uncon-
scious into the sand. I was dabbing my bleeding
mouth with the edge of my singlet, and wondering
what to do with Bert, when the steward and the
two deck officers came by on their way back to the
ship.

'Jesus Christ!' said one of them. 'What have you
done to your mate?' We got him back to the ship and
put him in his bunk. When he woke up the next day
he didn't remember anything about it all.

We didn't go near the trading post again, and up to
about one hour before we sailed three days later we
were under the impression that we'd managed to
cheat the Chinaman out of the money for the beer,
cigarettes, etcetera. Then just as we were congratulat-
ing ourselves a sailor came down from the bridge and
said, 'The Old Man wants you two on the bridge.'

When we got there the captain was there with our
chits in his hand talking to the Chinaman.

'Which one of you is Dean Swift?'

'Dean who, sir?'

He sighed, 'If you keep me arguing here while my
ship is preparing to leave port I'll log you a month's

110

pay each for endangering the ship. Which one of you is Dean Swift?'

Bert said, 'Me sir, it was just a joke . . .'

'And you are?'

'I'm Lloyd George, sir.'

The AB who was standing by to take the wheel laughed and Captain Mulligan could barely repress a smile which would probably have been his first.

'Well,' he said, 'you'll probably be delighted to know that I am going to pay your debts to the man and deduct it from your payoff at the termination of the voyage.'

'Thank you very much, sir.'

'Thank you, captain.'

'And the bosun will give you some paint and brushes and you'll paint the ship every night from here to Saigon.'

I said, 'Excuse me, sir, but it wasn't your chit we used for buying the beer, it was our own chits, wasn't it sir?'

The captain removed his cap and mopped the perspiration from his face and neck. The first mate came on to the bridge, 'All ready to cast off, sir.' He looked enquiringly from us to the Chinaman. 'Trouble, Captain?'

'Yes, Mister, Lloyd George and Dean Swift here insist on endangering my ship.'

'Er . . . Lloyd George, sir? Dean Swift, sir . . . ?'

'Oh Christ!' said the captain. 'Just get these people off my bridge, put the Chink ashore and let's put to sea, shall we?'

That evening after we'd finished work the bosun came along with two tins of white paint and some brushes.

'Captain's orders, lads, turn to and get painting. He says you can paint the deckhouse round your cabin and if you do a good job he'll forget about the rest.'

We painted our hearts out till it was too dark to see what we were doing. During the night we passed leeward of a tropic island and in the morning the wet paint was covered with a selection of moths and locusts and butterflies that would have delighted the heart of an entomologist.

But it didn't delight us, because we had to scrape it all off and do it again.

CHAPTER 6

One of the things peculiar to tramp steamers was the time spent in unsocial places waiting for the owners to find a cargo.

I used to imagine a couple of clerks working in one of those shipping offices in Leadenhall Street in the City of London. The mahogany and plate-glass halls of commerce smelling of ink and polish where I often delivered messages when I was a district messenger. One of these clerks opens his *Lloyd's Shipping Gazette* over tea and biscuits one morning.

'I see the *Innismoor* has arrived in Durban, Hawthorne. Have we got a cargo for her when she's empty?'

'Are you sure it's the *Innismoor*, Cranford? I thought she went down off Sydney a month ago.'

'No, that was her sister ship the *Nevernomore*, the galley boy went mad and opened the seacocks, they said it was all the rice and tinned rabbit that caused it, too rich for 'em.'

'Tell you what, cable the skipper to berth her over at the free moorings by the whaling station, we'll sort her out a cargo after the holidays.'

'But that's two weeks away, old boy, won't the crew be driven barmy by the stink of whale blubber and the biggest carnivorous flies in the world?'

'Very likely. Did I tell you about the greenfly on my roses? Heart-breaking old chap . . . heart-breaking.'

113

So a fortnight later, 'Heads she comes to London with a cargo of oranges or tails she takes coal to Sebang, then she can pop up to Saigon for some rice for Le Havre . . . tails it is, that's the *Innismoor* taken care of.'

'But supposing the rice crop is not ready when they get there?'

'Well they can take her up river into the jungle and swing at anchor for a week or so. They won't mind, hearts of oak those lads.'

So it came to pass that the *Innismoor* sailed up the river to Saigon past the mudflats and the paddyfields until, by a feat of superb navigation in the fading light of evening, the captain found a spot that looked more uninviting and fever ridden than the rest, and dropped anchor.

That night we leaned on the rail and listened to the brown muddy water sloshing along the sides of the ship and gloomily stared at the silhouettes of the trees on the banks about a hundred yards away. Occasionally a sampan visible by its oil lamps swinging and audible by the catfight conversations of the occupants glided past in the darkness.

At about ten o'clock a light warm rain fell for about an hour as it was to do almost every night and then when the rain stopped the air hummed and whined and pinged with the clouds of mosquitoes that obviously had never had a decent drink of blood in their lives until we turned up.

Sleep, with the stifling humidity and the door and portholes closed against the mosquitoes, was almost impossible. And hardly had I managed to doze off when Bert's voice from the bottom bunk jerked me back again.

114

'Blondie,' he was saying, 'I can hear voices, girls' voices.' He was given to occasionally talking in his sleep, but he generally stopped if you answered him.

'Of course you can,' I replied in a tone as kindly as I could manage. 'Now go to sleep, you soppy sod.'

'Listen,' he said.

I listened. Now I too could hear voices coming from outside on the deck, little sing-song giggling voices. Is it possible, I thought, that we have both gone mad at exactly the same time? Perhaps it was something in the food. Perhaps the weevils were getting their own back. Bert was by now out of his bunk and had switched on the light.

'Come on,' he said. 'Let's have a butcher's hook.'

When we got on deck we could see in the light from our doorway and the bulkhead lights on the well-deck that a large sampan was tied up alongside aft, and gathered on the deck near it was a little knot of about eight people; one, towering above them all, was obviously a man, large and muscular, dressed only in a pair of shorts and a circular, conical straw hat.

When he spotted us he padded lithely across to the foot of the ladder leading up to the after poop-deck where we were standing. And looking up, 'You like girl?' he asked in a loud whisper. Some of his companions had followed him and we could now see that they were indeed girls, little doll-like girls mostly dressed in black pyjama trousers and sandals and coloured tops.

'Jesus Christ,' said Bert, his voice hoarse with emotion. 'It's a floating whore shanty, look at 'em, ain't they beautiful?' I looked down at the lovely smiling oriental faces.

'Well, I don't suppose the bloody Seamen's Mission

sent 'em, and we haven't got five bob between us, so what's the good of looking?' I replied dolefully.

The big coolie must have sensed the gist of my remark and he grunted and turned away.

'Hold on,' said Bert. 'What about all that junk we got in Sebang? Let's try him with it.' And to the coolie, 'Oi Johnny! No money, plenty lighters, penknives and cigarettes.' We still had the cigarettes because they were impossible to smoke, they burned like those sparklers you get on Guy Fawkes night.

The man bounded up the ladder followed by some of the girls. 'Me see,' he grunted, pointing to a very humourless eye set in a brown pockmarked face. It was now apparent that he wore a curved sword like those you see in films about the Japanese samurai. The girls crowded into our little cabin after him, they were mostly small and delicate looking with light brown complexions and dark mischievous eyes. The man said something in their own language which must have meant 'belt up' because except for the occasional giggle they became silent.

I dragged our cardboard box of treasures from beneath the bottom bunk and held it out for his inspection. One of the girls picked up a lighter and said something which made them all laugh, even the coolie, then he told them to belt up again.

'What do you say, Johnny?' I said. 'Four lighters, four penknives and two cartons of fags for two girls?' He whistled thoughtfully through his gold front teeth. I could see that Bert had already got his hand up the blouse of a delectable little doll in the corner, and she wasn't by any means putting up a struggle, so I slipped my free arm round the nearest who could have been her sister.

116

'Here, take the bloody lot,' I said, 'and don't come back before the morning, OK?'

Without a change of expression he took the box from me, grunted, shoved the rest of his brood out through the doorway and closed the door behind him.

We must have dozed off to be awakened sometime later by a voice booming, 'What the hell are all these people doing on my ship?! Watchman! Where's the bloody watchman? Get these natives over the side and cast off that sampan!' I slapped the warm little body beside me in the top bunk. She seemed to know what was expected, and with a squeal and a giggle grabbed her clothes from the foot of the bunk and, followed by her sister, slipped out into the night.

Unfortunately they forgot to close the door behind them and we awoke in the morning almost disfigured by insect bites; but we were smiling, at least, I think we were.

One afternoon a few days later I was sitting in the sunshine by number two hatch watching the sacks of rice going down the hold, when Bert came out of the galley with his after dinner mug of tea and sat down beside me.

'Here Blondie,' he said, in a low conspiratorial voice hardly audible above the clanking of the winches and the shouts of the stevedores, 'd'you know what the donkeyman told me? He said that you can buy opium here for about ten bob a pound.' He gave me a knowing look and buried his face in his mug.

I said, 'Ain't you bleeding dopey enough without smoking opium?'

His face emerged and he gave me a withering glance. 'We don't smoke it, you bloody fool, we sell it in England and make a fortune.'

I said, 'Don't you know that if they catch us smuggling opium we'll get about five years in the nick? That donkeyman is determined to drop us in it, isn't he? Only yesterday he was trying to kid us to go up to town to the Barracks and join the French Foreign Legion.'

He grinned. 'That would have been funny, wouldn't it? Especially like old Cooky says, it's a punishment battalion. Imagine me and you galloping through the jungle with a sack of stones on our backs; here, here's you.'

He got to his feet, swung a half empty sack of rice over his shoulder, and went lolloping around the deck doing an imitation of me crying for my mother and begging for mercy. His feet skidded on the loose rice that was everywhere and the coolies screamed with laughter as his feet went skywards and he landed on his back. He rose painfully, gave the coolies a black look, and resumed his seat alongside me on a pile of hatch covers.

'Those bastards have got a nerve laughing at a white man,' he growled.

I was nearly helpless myself.

'Are you going to sit there giggling like some tart all day or do you want me to tell you about this opium?'

'All right, tell me about the opium.'

'Well the donkeyman says that if we can flog a couple of pounds of opium in London we'd get enough money to live like little lords for a whole year, birds, booze, the lot.'

I must say that I found the notion of living like little lords for a whole year very appealing indeed, but, 'We won't get much birds and booze if we get caught by the customs and get five years in Dartmoor,' I said.

118

Bert finished his tea and stood up. 'Come with me,' he said. 'I'll show you a hiding place where nobody would think of looking, come on.'

I followed him up the iron ladder to our cabin. When we were inside, he said, 'Now, if you were going to hide something in here where would you put it? Take your time.'

I said, 'I'd probably put it in your bunk, it's a brave customs man who disturbs some of the things that must be living in that mattress.'

'No, seriously,' he said, 'where would you put it? You don't know do you? Well watch this.'

He pushed the door open, and after a glance round outside to see if anyone was looking, took from his pocket a small screwdriver and proceeded to remove the screws holding the strip of brass across the top of the breakwater, the high wooden step that is beneath the doors of all deck cabins to stop the waves coming in.

'How about that?' he asked proudly, pointing into the cavity beneath the brass, a hollow about a foot deep and three inches wide. 'Now am I a bloody genius or am I not?'

However, as is so often the case, genius was to go unrewarded and as it proved eventually just as well.

Whether it was true about the opium we never did find out because investing in the future is all very well, but, when home is so very far away, who can tell when you're going to get your next bottle of beer or meet another girl who might cry if you don't go home with her and meet her mattress? And these things do cost money, wherever you may be, but nevertheless are a wiser option than buying opium.

Because it came to pass that some weeks later the

Innismoor entered the Bristol Channel on her way to Barry Dock. We were in the cabin sorting out any things that we owned that might be worth taking home again, when, knock! knock! at the door. The door opened and a round chubby-cheeked Welsh customs officer entered.

'Good afternoon, gentlemen, His Majesty's Customs and Excise. Don't mind me, just carry on.'

He produced a folding yardstick and a torch from his bag and commenced to tap the bulkheads and shine his torch behind pipes and in crevices. He flipped Bert's suitcase open and flipped it shut again.

'You've come from the Far East?' More a statement than a question. Tap – Tap – Tap!

'Yes, from Saigon.'

'A good voyage?' Tap – Tap – Tap!

'Not bad, we were on fire in number two hold going into Le Havre.'

'Yes, you were carrying rice, weren't you? A bit tricky that, they say if you put the hose on it it swells up and splits your ship open, and that wouldn't do, would it now?'

I said, 'A bloody good riddance as far as I'm concerned.'

He chuckled. 'She's not a very nice ship, is she boyo? Now will one of you be so kind as to hold the door open for me while I have a little peek under here?'

He took a small screwdriver from his case and removed the brass strip on the breakwater, shone his torch inside the cavity, measured it inside and out, and replaced the metal strip.

'Well better luck next time, isn't it? Cheerio, lads.'

'Cheerio.'

CHAPTER 7

After that voyage Bert and I never did go to sea together again. In fact we rarely saw each other. He made himself comfortable on the Cunard passenger liners on the North Atlantic run to Canada and America, while I, with some variations, spent the next three years backwards and forwards to Brazil and the River Plate.

Although I lived at home in between voyages during the early part of that period, I always spent as little time in the house as possible. It was becoming a very unhappy place. My mother was by now a confirmed alcoholic. And although my sister came home occasionally from the TB sanatorium, the conditions at home were too much for her and in the end the doctors wouldn't let her leave the sanatorium until she was well a long time later.

Each time I saw my father when I came home he had changed. Eventually he no longer shouted, 'Jesus Christ!' and offered to fight the world when things went wrong for him. Now he muttered, 'Oh dear, oh dear.' And sat bowed and crumpled with his face in his hands.

One day when I was about nineteen I returned from Australia to find the house locked and empty. The curtains had gone from the windows and the inside was dark and bare. Mrs Haynes from next door was across the road talking to Mrs Lyons.

'They've moved,' she said, 'gone away three weeks ago. Didn't you know?'

I said, 'Yes, I must have forgotten.'

'Somewhere in St Mary Cray, Orpington way. I think Mrs Finch at forty-six has got the address,' she went on.

'Thanks, I won't trouble at the moment. Goodbye.'

'Goodbye, Dennis.'

If I remember my emotions at that moment in time I don't seem to recall any great sorrow at this parting of the ways, as such it was. I had never been close to my parents, and on the occasions when I spent time in their company we were so intolerant of each other as to be best apart. So I don't suppose any tears were shed on either side.

That evening I left my suitcase with Moss Wallace, the proprietor of the Jubilee Café in Deptford Bridge Road, and slept the night in Carrington House, an LCC doss house just around the corner from the café. It wasn't the first time I'd slept in such a place, and I knew the drill of putting a leg of the bed in each of my shoes and my clothes under the mattress so that they would be safe from any sportsman angling with a bent safety pin on a bit of string over the top of the cubicle during the night. The bedclothes were rough to the touch but clean, and the coughs and snores and night noises of the other men were no more than you'd get in the average ship's fo'c'sle, so for ninepence a night you couldn't grumble. In the morning, awakened by one of the custodians gently banging two dustbin lids together, I made my way back to Moss Wallace's for a wash and breakfast.

I had been a frequenter of the Jubilee Café between voyages for quite some time and I knew Moss Wallace perhaps better than I did my father – and liked him more. Moss was a big barrel of a man, an ex-policeman, a kind man with a twinkling eye and an absurd sense of fun, who described himself as 'An ex-copper, thirty years on the beat and never got a conviction.' He had a great booming voice and was given to standing behind his counter and announcing, 'It's a Pigmalian affair!' or it might be, 'A Dog-malian affair!' or, 'A Catmalian affair!' in a voice that would cause his customers to choke on their chips and spill their tea in their laps, loud enough to dismay passers-by and frighten the horses in the street outside. He would re-enact fragments of mythical court cases for the bewilderment of any occupant of the café who didn't know him, and for his own amusement. Suddenly he would put down the cup he was wiping and take the oath solemnly on a greasy menu, then standing stiffly to attention, 'Your Worship,' he would boom, 'at twelve twenty-seven on the night of the twenty-eighth I was proceeding along the High Street when I noticed the accused up an alley killing a pig without a licence. When I informed him that he was under arrest he replied, "Who, me?" And I was forced to kick the crap out of him for his own protection. That, m'lud, is the case for the prosecution.' Or he would suddenly drape a dishcloth over his head to simulate the wig, become a judge, and solemnly pronounce, 'George Arthur Pushcart, you are hereby sentenced to seven years' hard labour for riding a bike without a light and if you die before your time your father will have to serve it for you. Take him down.'

That morning after I'd eaten I helped Moss with a few little jobs because his wife was away, and at eleven o'clock I said, 'They're open Moss, I'm going over the Crown for a pint, shall I bring you back a bottle?'

He said, 'No, I'll come with you.'

There were no customers in the café but at that moment two down-and-outs from Carrington House walked in. The first man put threepence on the counter. 'Two teas, please.' Moss drew himself up, inflated his fifty-inch chest, and fixed them with his policeman's eye. 'Thirty years,' he boomed, 'thirty years I walked the beat, out in all weathers, rain and shine, slush and sleet just to save enough money to buy this place.' He paused, and they nodded their appreciation for his sacrifice. 'And you,' he continued, 'come in here, throwing your money about, demanding instant service. This gentleman,' indicating me, 'has been in here since last Wednesday and he hasn't been served yet, so what chance have you got?'

By now they were thoroughly bewildered. One of them picked up the threepence and muttered something about going somewhere else. Moss leaned forward across the counter. 'I think you're very wise,' he said in a low voice. And taking a perfectly clean cup off the shelf held it up for their inspection. 'Look at the state of that! Would you drink out of that?'

Without pausing to give their opinion they practically made a run for the open door. A moment later when Moss was turning the key in the door from the outside another would-be customer approached.

'You're not closed, are you?'

'Only temporary, sir, can't touch a thing until the murder squad have been.'

I've mentioned Moss Wallace because, looking back, I think it was his wonderful sense of the ridiculous that planted the seed in me that so many years later led me on to becoming a writer of comedy.

I was as they say 'on the beach' for a long time after returning from Australia. I would have liked to have gone back in the same ship when she turned round, but I'd got the sack in London following an incident in Sydney where, in a moment of pique, I had clouted the cook with a frying-pan full of hot fat. Most of the crew agreed that he was about due for a short sharp lesson, and that when he came out of hospital he was a better person for it. But I got the sack just the same.

For the next month or so I slept the nights in Carrington House and spent most of the days hanging around the Jubilee Café, occasionally helping out for a meal and a packet of Woodbines and maybe sixpence to go to the pictures. Sometimes I went over to the Shipping Federation to look for a ship and sometimes I went totting with Stan the Coalman, another habitué of the Jubilee Café. Stan the Coalman wasn't really a coalman, he was a rag and bone man. It was said that he was called Stan the Coalman because it was such a long time since he had a wash he always looked as though he'd just been delivering some coal.

Stan was a diddicoy. About the same age as myself, he was dark like a gypsy, and when he spoke his conversation was economical and spiced with Romany words and phrases. He rarely smiled and on the odd occasion that he allowed his dirty face the luxury of a grin his eyes seldom lacked their gamut of expressions which ranged from suspicion to mistrust. Winter and summer he wore a long black greasy overcoat and a dirty tweed cap pulled down over one ear, and behind the other ear he always kept a cigarette butt which was never smoked. In fact there was a consensus of opinion that it was always the same

125

dog-end and it had been there for years and he'd forgotten it was there. Knotted round his neck he sported a red bandanna kerchief which he kept straightening and loosening and tightening as he sucked air through the gap in his front teeth when he was thinking.

Totting with Stan was always an interesting way of passing a few hours, with generally a couple of pints of beer and maybe half a crown at the end of the day if he did well. His horse was a sturdy brown and white animal, always very full of himself, always prancing about and showing off, and Stan would talk to him all the time, 'just to remind him who is the guv'nor.' 'Behave yourself,' he would growl constantly. 'Behave yourself, you silly bastard.' Sometimes when we were in an open space like Blackheath Stan would let the reins relax and wave his cap in the air and shout, 'Go on! Go on, my son!' And we'd go charging along in the little coster's cart like two gladiators, Stan sitting in the driver's seat and me standing behind him hanging on for dear life. Then Stan would take control, heaving on the reins and shouting, 'All right, all right, you've had your fun, now behave yourself, behave yourself.' And the horse's ears would twitch and he'd gradually settle down to a trot again.

I remember the first time I went out with Stan the coalman as a very enlightening experience. We were going totting around Blackheath Village.

'What sort of things are we going to buy?' I asked in all innocence.

'Buy?' He said 'buy' as though he'd never heard the word before. 'I'm not going to buy anything. I haven't come all this way to give money away, mush. I'm a totter, not an effing missionary.'

126

'Oh, well what sort of things are we going to collect?'

'That's more like it, a bit of brass, a bit of lead, a bit of copper. Perhaps some old furniture if it's worth me while carting it away. Horse hair is fetching a good price lately.'

Then he said, 'But there's no need for you to go worrying your head about all that, if there's any talking leave it to me, all right mush?'

That morning our first customer appeared almost as soon as Stan started his chant, 'Ragandbonesoldlumber!' She was a neatly dressed white-haired old lady who emerged from the doorway of a cottage on the outskirts of the village. She tripped down the garden path and waved from the gateway.

'Young man! Young man!'

Stan stopped the cart and climbed down. He touched the peak of his cap. 'Good mornin', missus.'

'Good morning, young man. I wonder if you'd be interested in a very nice sofa that I'm having to get rid of?'

Stan sucked his teeth thoughtfully, 'Just a sofa, missus, nothing more?'

The little old lady shook her head. 'I'm sorry,' she replied, 'that is really all I've got for you, it's such a nice sofa, the milkman said anyone would give me at least a pound for it.'

'Then why don't he give you a pound for it? I hope it's not a very big one, I don't want to fill the cart up before I've started, do I?'

'Oh,' her happy enthusiasm was replaced by a pensive frown. 'I'm afraid it's rather large,' she said apologetically. 'That is the reason I'm having to get rid of it. Perhaps you'd come in and have a look and

127

see what you think.' She opened the garden gate invitingly. I was dying to remind Stan that it might be made of horse hair, a point he seemed to have forgotten, but he had said he would do all the talking, so it would be his loss not mine, and serve him right, the bloody fool. Stan stood sucking his teeth and looking both ways up the road like a man seeking escape from old ladies trying to sell him sofas. Then at last, 'All right, lady,' he said grudgingly, 'we'll have a look at it.'

Thank Christ, now he is beginning to show some sense! The little front room of the cottage smelt of polish and lavendar and was crowded with furniture. Another old lady almost identical to the first was sitting in an armchair by the fire, knitting.

'This is my sister,' said our one. 'Since she lost her husband and moved in with me we've had to let a few of our things go, we just haven't got room for them.'

The little old lady by the fire smiled and Stan touched his cap and I nodded sympathetically.

'This is it,' she continued, indicating a great black shiny sofa that took up most of the far side of the room under the window.

'You can see that it really is a very nice sofa and why the milkman thought it was worth at least a pound, can't you young man?'

Not answering, Stan sighed and threaded his way through the maze of occasional tables, cake stands, aspidistras and knick-knacks. Then, reaching the settee, he tweaked his forefinger and thumb into a tiny rent in the side and pulled forth a morsel of stuffing.

'Just as I thought,' he grunted, 'horse hair.' The disgust in his voice couldn't have been more apparent if he had said, 'It's full of horse shit.'

**Saigon 1934. Would you buy a girl off
this man? I did.**

The old lady by now was getting very depressed about the whole thing. 'Perhaps I could take a bit less for it as it's horse hair,' she said hopefully. 'Perhaps I could take ten shillings. I'm sure the milkman didn't know it was a horse hair settee.'

Stan fiddled with his kerchief and sucked his teeth, his dark eyes darting round the contents of the room.

'He knew all right,' he said without looking at her. 'He was just having you on, missus, just having you on he was, the rascal.'

By now the little old lady had really lost her bearings. Her settee had turned out to be full of horse shit, or the equivalent, and her friend the milkman had purposely led her into making a laughing stock of herself.

'I shall give him a good ticking off in the morning,' she chirped.

'Yes, you do that, missus,' said Stan examining a vase off one of the little tables and mentally spitting on it and putting it back again. He straightened his red kerchief again and sighed. 'I don't know what we can do for you, missus,' he said hopelessly. 'I just don't know what we can do. Do you know what we can do, Spikey boy?'

'No I don't, Stan,' I replied. I had not really quite recovered from the shock of the sudden collapse of the horse hair market.

'Even he doesn't know what we can do,' he said, waving a hopeless grimy palm in my direction.

'I could take five shillings,' she said nervously. 'I could take five shillings, couldn't I Martha?'

The other little old lady didn't wish to be involved so she said nothing. Stan ignored the latest price reduction.

'I know what he wants to do,' he indicated me again, 'he wants to leave you with it, that's what he wants to do. But I am not going to let him do that, no missus I am not.' The old lady looked scornfully at me over her glasses. The circle of people she could trust in this world was narrowing rapidly, thank God for good old Stan.

'Half a crown,' said Stan suddenly. 'Half a tosheroon and you're rid of the sofa if you'd like to chuck in those old brass fire irons in the corner there.' He indicated a set of heavy gleaming brass fire irons, poker, shovel, tongs and brush, hanging on their stand under a writing desk in another corner of the room. The old lady ran a thin worried hand across her wrinkled brow.

'I didn't really want to . . .' she began.

'Well, that's it, missus, isn't it?' Stan broke in. 'I'm trying to do you a favour and you're wasting my time. We're busy fellers we are, we can't stand here all day. I can't do better than that so I'll say good day to you.'

He touched the peak of his cap to them both and turned towards the door, but before he reached it, she said sadly, 'All right then, I suppose it's all right.'

When we were loading the settee on the cart, I said, 'You're a hard hearted bleeder, Stan.'

He preened himself for a moment and smiled a little smile. 'You think so? Let's go back and get the bits of brass. I'm not finished yet, am I?'

The old lady had brought the fire irons out on to the step. 'You haven't forgotten the half a crown?' she asked plaintively.

Stan shook his head, 'Not me lady, never forget money, can't afford to can I?' And held out his hand.

She looked as perplexed as I was. 'No,' she said. 'You owe me half a crown.'

Stan looked hurt. 'Do you know something, lady?' he said, with quiet sincerity. 'D'you know something, I've never owed a penny in my life, on my mother's grave I haven't; no dear, you've got it all wrong, you promised us half a crown and the old fire irons for carting the old sofa away, we can't cart it away for nothing, can we now?'

She stood for a moment trying to fathom out how her mind could have been playing her such tricks.

'I tell you what lady, make it two bob and we'll all be happy.'

When she came back with her purse, Stan said, 'Oh I'm sorry to trouble you lady, but do you think you could let me have a bucket of water for the horse?'

She found us a galvanized iron bucket which Stan filled from the tap in the garden.

When we got back to the cart Stan flipped me the two shilling piece and said, 'Here Spikey, you go over to the pub and get us a couple of pints and some bread and cheese while I water the horse and put his nosebag on.'

I felt like saying, 'No, I don't want any part of the two bob you conned off the old lady.' But I was hungry. Later, when we'd come out of the pub and we were going up the road I noticed the bucket in the back of the cart. I said, 'Stan, we've still got the old girl's bucket in the back here.'

He looked back from where he was leading the horse. 'Have we?' he said in mock surprise. 'Don't tell me you've nicked the old lady's bucket, Spikey. I'm ashamed of you, you're worse than I am, you are.'

Occasionally during this period, which was of

about six or seven weeks, the longest I'd ever been 'on the beach', I tried for a shore job. But there were plenty of people looking for jobs, and however much I lied about settling down and joining the pension fund, employers were loath to employ a merchant seaman who would probably give them and their factory a 'sailor's farewell' as soon as the boat came in.

Once I borrowed a pick and shovel off one of the habitués of the Jubilee Café and bluffed my way on to the building site as a navvy, but I hadn't been there more than an hour when the owner of the pick and shovel arrived to say he himself had got to start on another site and demanded his tools back, leaving me standing in a shallow depression which I had hoped would some day become a trench. The foreman was an observant man, and it didn't take him long to observe that I was now the only navvy on the site digging with a piece of wood and his bare hands, and I was out of work almost before I'd started.

By the time my luck changed and I signed on the *Highland Princess* back to Brazil and the River Plate things had reached the stage where my friends were risking their lives crossing busy roads when they saw me coming, and drinking in pubs they didn't like, to avoid me putting the bite on them for the price of a meal and/or ninepence for a night's kip. They say that it is at times like that you know who your friends are. I knew who my friends were all right, the trouble was I didn't know where they were.

'The moving finger writes,' said Omar Khayyam, 'and, having writ, moves on.' To be honest I have never quite understood what he meant by that but it seems a good, if desperate, way to end this chapter. And if I can think of a better way I'll do it again later.

CHAPTER 8

By the time Mr Chamberlain had put into practice his
hundred-per-cent surefire way of lousing up a Sunday morning, I had left the sea and was working as a
stevedore in the docks, which was my birthright as
the son of a stevedore. My first impulse on hearing the
words, 'We are now at war with Germany', was not so
much to fight for King and Country but to get the hell
out of it until they'd all got this thing out of their
systems. But as time went by and nothing seemed to
happen worse than an occasional siren or a flaming
barrage balloon struck by lightning, there seemed
little reason to do anything very drastic for the
moment.

About midsummer of 1940 something happened
that seemed, and indeed was, a very good reason to
stay put. I had been for some time lodging with a
family in Bermondsey. And when the husband got
called up for the Army because he was in the Territor-
ials, his wife and children decided to go and live with
some relations in the country. They could have taken
me with them, I'd have liked living in the country, but
they didn't.

I found my next lodgings with a young couple who
had a house in East Greenwich. She was about
twenty-five years of age. Her name was Beth and she
was pretty and vivacious. Her husband Charlie was
about the same age, a timber porter in the Surrey Dock

who spent more time in the pub than he did at home. They rowed almost constantly. Once he hit her, and two of her brothers who were stevedores like myself came over and beat him up.

One afternoon I finished work early and made my way home after the pubs closed. Beth was there, she was very unhappy as she so often was these days. When I walked in she was standing at the sink in the scullery washing her face and neck with a flannel. Her dress was open as far as it would go. She said, 'Hello Spike, I wasn't expecting you. I'm just having a rinse.'

I said, 'Have you been crying again? Your eyes are all red.' Suddenly she was crying on my shoulder. It was a hot summer day and she wore hardly anything under the little cotton frock, and when I kissed her her lips were soft and salty with tears. Somewhat shakily I said, 'Er, I'm going up to have a lay down for an hour.' She buried her head in my shoulder and in a muffled, hardly audible voice murmured, 'With me?'

From then we made love every time we were given the chance, afternoons, evenings, lunchtime, anytime. And the more perilous the time and the situation the more we enjoyed it. Once we managed it while he was down the street getting some ice cream. The blitz came and we made love on the mattress in the Anderson shelter at the bottom of the garden, often frantic 'we might not be here tomorrow' love, while bombs were falling and the smell of burning houses drifted through the sacks and blankets over the doorway.

But alas all good things, as they say, come to an end. And the end of that particular good thing came when one afternoon Beth and I were giggling our way down the stairs as her husband unexpectedly walked in the front door. Unfortunately my boots and her dress were still in the kitchen where today's action had started, and it didn't need a Sherlock Holmes to deduce that we hadn't been upstairs cleaning the windows.

'Oh my God!' said Beth, and bolted upstairs again even faster than she'd gone up there an hour previously.

'You've been knocking off my old woman, haven't you?' said Charlie. I descended the rest of the stairs.

'Now wait a minute . . .' I can't for the life of me think what he was supposed to wait for, unless it was my disappearance through the front door which was still open behind him. But Charlie had no intention of waiting, and a big fist came looping across and caught me above the right eye closing that side down almost immediately.

I think it was a pity that when Beth told me that Charlie was impotent she hadn't mentioned the fuss he would make about something he hadn't got any use for. Within minutes there was a lot of blood about, most of it mine. Luckily Beth's screeching out of the top window and the crowd of neighbours in the doorway attracted the attention of a passing police-man who came in and stopped it before someone got killed, probably me.

When all was quietened down I went and threw my few things into my suitcase. I'd twigged it was moving day. When I went into the kitchen to get my boots, he was seated in the fire-side chair and she was dabbing his face with a piece of rag in a bowl of water. Neither of them spoke so I didn't say anything either. I suppose it was best that way.

That night I spent down the communal air-raid shelter in Greenwich Park, and in the morning decided that there didn't seem a lot to hang around for so I might as well get myself a ship and go somewhere, maybe Australia and stay there.

There was the usual crowd in the Shipping Federation but nobody I knew, so I sat down on one of the benches to wait and see what was happening. Seated next to me was an old man, probably one of those who, too old to go to sea anymore, hang about such places because they enjoy the company of seafaring men and maybe get a couple of pints of beer and some tobacco now and again. When I'd rolled a cigarette I offered him the pouch and papers. He proceeded to roll a cigarette like a young cigar.

'You just back?' he asked.

I said, 'No, I've been ashore for a while and I want to get away again.'

He looked at me with surprise and chuckled. 'You've picked a fine time for it,' he said, as he lit his giant roll-up. 'Half of this lot have just been fished out of the drink within the last couple of weeks or so, mines, the Estuary and the Channel are full of 'em. They talk about nothing else down here lately.'

At that moment the Federation Officer opened the hatch and called, 'Anyone for the *Jervis Bay*, signing this afternoon?' A few men drifted across to the hatch.

I said, 'I think I'll take a chance on her, she might be going to the Colonies, she used to in peacetime, didn't she?' and started to get to my feet. He laid a horny hand on my arm and said in a slightly shocked tone of voice, 'You're never going away in her? She'll go to Davy Jones Locker, that's where she's going.'

I was becoming a bit depressed and annoyed at this old shell-back and his bleating. 'For Chrissake, some

136

of 'em must get past the mines, mustn't they?' I asked peevishly.

He sighed and pushed his whiskery face close to my ear. 'She's an armed merchant cruiser.' When he saw the information meant nothing to me, he leaned forward again. 'Supposing your convoy runs into one of these pocket battleships, you've heard of them haven't you, son?'

'Yes.'

'Supposing you meet up with one of them, she is the one who has got to stay and fight while the rest of them get away. She's got no chance. Stay off her, if you'll take my advice.'

Now I was in a bit of a quandary. The thought of going back to sea hadn't thrilled me much in the first place and the idea of getting dumped in the ocean appealed to me even less. I recalled what my mate Pat Greenaway on the *Highland Princess* had told me about when he was wrecked in the *Highland Hope*, and it didn't seem something you put your name down for.

No, I hadn't come this far to be drowned nor blown up by a pocket battleship. I'd think of something else, although I mustn't take too long about it or I might find myself called up in the Army, and the only person who seemed to think the Army was a great life was the bloke who did the posters.

On the bus going back to Deptford sitting a few seats away from me was a thickset middle-aged man in RAF uniform, and as I idly looked at him, I suddenly got to thinking that this fellow had got it all worked out. He'd got a nice uniform, looked well fed, and he probably got paid as well, and he didn't have to dig trenches or run around with a bayonet like the

137

Army did. On the impulse of the moment I went and sat on the empty seat beside him.

'Excuse me mate, this RAF thing that you're in, what's it like?'

He fixed me with a very solid eye. 'In the first place,' he said coldly, 'I am not called "mate" I am called Flight Sergeant,' indicating three stripes surmounted by a gold crown on his sleeve. 'What do you think this is, Scotch mist? And secondly I am not in the RAF thing, I am serving in the Royal Air Force.'

'All right then, Flight Sergeant,' I said patiently. 'What's it like in the Royal Air Force?'

He surveyed my freshly stitched countenance for a few moments with some distaste. 'It's a good life if you can take it, and if they'll have you, it'll make a man of you.'

I said, 'How do you join?'

'Go to your local recruiting office, they'll sort you out. I get off here, good luck.'

I stood up to let him pass and I said, 'Good luck, mate.'

He hesitated long enough to give me the cold, beady-eyed, head-to-toe look that I was to become so familiar with from flight sergeants over the next few years, and left.

A few days later the officer at RAF Station Uxbridge flipped through the pile of papers I had accumulated since nine o'clock that morning, leaned back in his chair and banged the tips of his fingers together.

'Well, old chap, you seem to have come through quite well. Afraid aircrew is out, you might have been considered for air gunner but there is a bit of a weakness in the right eye.'

That's a relief!

My Merchant Navy discharge book was clipped to the papers. He picked it up and ruffled through its pages stamped with the names and destinations of the ships I'd sailed on over the last few years.

'What's wrong with the Merchant Navy, don't they want you back?'

'I've tried, sir, but they haven't got any ships, the Germans have sunk 'em all.'

Another officer at the trestle table went, 'Tch, Tch!' and said, 'Careless talk man, careless talk.' I thought, there's hundreds of them down the Federation talking about nothing else, but I didn't say anything.

'They tell me,' he continued, 'you want to be inducted immediately. Bloody funny that, everyone else can't wait to bugger off home again. Good man, good man.' He opened the discharge book at the last page with a discharge on it and hit it with a big red rubber stamp which said, 'Enlisted in Royal Air Force for the Duration of Emergency. Officer I/C Records Attestation Station Uxbridge Mddx,' and signed it.

'You are now Aircraftman Second Class, Number one two nine o eight two four. Don't forget that number, from now on you won't get permission to cough without it. Good luck to you. Sergeant, find this man a billet!'

I followed the sergeant out of the room and as we were going through the passage I said, 'Well, that's a relief,' and got my cigarettes out.

He shouted, 'No talking! Put them cigarettes away. Get your hand out of your pocket, and follow me!'

I thought, 'Christ! What have I done now?'

The following twenty-four hours was a blurred kaleidoscope of impressions of clothing stores.

'Kitbags one!'

139

'Tunics two!'
'Trousers two!'
'Overalls one!'
'Buttonsticks one!'
'Boots pairs two!'
'Housewives one!'
'Follow me!'
'No talking!'

A barrack room with beds and lockers and blue blankets, crowded with young men, writing, writing.

'Get fell in outside with mugs and eating irons! Don't forget your gas masks!'

Crowded bustling dining halls.

'If my old woman gave me this to eat I'd throw it at her.'

'Don't you want it? Give it to me I'll eat it, thanks mate.'

'I say old boy, you don't actually like that garbage, do you?'

'How would you like a knuckle sandwich?'

'Sorry I spoke, won't speak again.'

'Good.'

Lines of men on the barrack square with kitbags and pith-helmets.

'Where they going Sarge'?'

'Bloody Norway I shouldn't be surprised.'

'Here's some brown paper and string, make a neat parcel of your civvies and address it to where you want it to go.'

Night in the barrack room. Men still writing, writing. Men in little groups. Quiet conversation. Mostly serious conversations.

'I don't know what I'm doing here, deferred for a year they said, and that was last week.'

'What about me? Exempt I was. My guv'nor wrote to them personally, can't run the firm without me. I'll be out within a week, you see if I'm not.'

'Here's the sergeant, let's ask him if we can have a twenty-four hour pass.'

They've only just got here, what do they want to go home for?

'Sergeant, whom do we ask about a twenty-four hour pass?'

'You can ask whom you like son, you won't get one.'

'Can we go down the town and have a drink?'

'Not in our bloody uniform you don't, we've still got some pride left.'

'Can they make us stay here, like this?'

'You're in the mob now son, they can make you do anything. They can make you have a baby if they like, and the only satisfaction you've got is that they can't make you love it.'

'But surely we're entitled . . .'

The voice becomes gritty and sharper. 'Entitled? Two things you're entitled to, you're entitled to twenty-four inches in the ranks and twenty-four square feet of bedspace, but you won't always get it. There's an officer approaching, stand by your beds. Attention!'

A rather elderly officer strolls through the doorway. The sergeant salutes, rigidly at attention, the officer salutes languidly.

'Everything all right, Sergeant?'

'Yessir, everything all right, sir.'

'Jolly good. I'll just have a few words. All right men, stand easy, relax. I didn't say sit on your bed. Take that man's name and number, Sergeant.'

141

'What's your name, that man?'

'Mullins, Sergeant.'

'Number?'

'One nine two, wait a minute, one two nine, er, I've got it written down here somewhere.'

'All right, Sergeant, sort that out later. Now tomorrow, you men will leave for RAF Station Bridgnorth, which is an RAF training camp . . .'

An air raid siren starts wailing nearby.

'Shall I take these men down the shelter, sir?'

'Not while I'm talking to them, Sergeant, you may go if you wish.'

The sergeant pouts but says nothing.

'As I was saying, Bridgnorth is an RAF training establishment where for the next six weeks you will be taught how to conduct yourselves as airmen in the Royal Air Force . . .' And on and on until he runs out of words. 'Carry on Sergeant.'

They exchange salutes and he leaves. The 'all clear' sounds.

I've found my piece of paper with the number on it.

'You want my number, Sergeant?'

'No forget it, I'm not putting anyone on a charge for that cocky bastard. Lights out in one hour, time to get them buttons and cap badges polished and clean your boots ready for parade in the morning. Goodnight.'

It is dark and somewhere someone is crying in his sleep. A siren sounds in the night, some bombs whistle down not far away and guns go 'Clump! Clump!' Somebody says, 'There's a raid on, what are we supposed to do?'

Matches scrape and flicker as cigarettes are lit. A Cockney voice says, 'You're in the bleedin' Air Force, get up there and shoot the bastards down, mate, I'm

142

gonna get some kip.' Soon it is all quiet again except for someone crying in his sleep.

When we got to Bridgnorth later the next afternoon we were shouted into a large hut with lockers and beds down either side and an iron pot-bellied stove in the centre, told to dump our gear on a bed and get fell in outside to go and eat. When we'd eaten we went back to the hut and sat around on the beds smoking and talking until from the doorway a voice barked, 'Stand by your beds! Put them cigarettes out! Come on, jump to it!'

The owner of the voice was a husky young man with a corporal's stripes on his arm wearing a white rollneck pullover under his tunic. He strode slowly down the centre of the room surveying us with insolent contempt.

'Do those buttons up. Stand to attention, heels together, thumbs in line with the seams of the trousers. That's more like it. Now let me introduce myself, my name is Corporal Williams. I am your drill instructor for the next six weeks, by which time I hope to be sergeant, and if I'm not I'll hold you bloody shower responsible. I am a regular, which means that I wasn't, like most of you lot, dragged in for the duration. That man there, why are you leaning on the bed? Are you a cripple? D'you want a wheelchair?'

'No.'

'No Corporal.'

'No Corporal.'

'As I was saying, I am a regular, and there is a saying in the Royal Air Force that the NCO regulars are the biggest bastards of the lot, and it's perfectly true, so watch out. So now you know about me. Let's find out a bit about you. You there, what do you do in Civvy Street?'

'I was a carpenter, Corporal.'

'You?'

'Salesman, Corporal.'

'You?'

'Merchant seaman, Corporal.'

'A merchant seaman, eh? We don't get many of them. Why did you join the Air Force?'

'Because I didn't want to get drowned.'

He laughed as if it was the funniest thing he'd heard in years, and when the corporal laughs, everybody laughs, and the hut dissolved into laughter.

From then on I was the golden boy, a novelty, a fellow to be regarded with a twinkle of the eye. A few days later he actually bought me a pint in the Naafi. And once when we were marching on the square the flight sergeant in charge of discipline, who was reckoned to be a bigger menace to the English speaking people than Hitler, roared, 'Smarten up those men, Corporal. They're like a lot of old women! Mind that puddle Mullins, we don't want to lose you!'

When the time came to leave Bridgnorth I think I was the only one of my entry who was sorry to go. I'd made a lot of friends, and the eternal spit and polish never worried me like it did some people. For thirty-four shillings a fortnight, and with nothing to buy but beer and fags, plenty of good food, and a bed with sheets, I'd have stayed there for ever. But alas all good things come to an end some time. And on the station notice board appeared a list of names under the heading 'Postings'. And there among them, 1290824 AC2 Mullins, D to 66 Squadron, RAF Station, Biggin Hill, Kent.

144

**With Halifax 'E. Eddie' 1943. Nobody
told me it was formal.**

CHAPTER 9

I arrived at Biggin Hill RAF Station one bleak November afternoon, and as I shouldered my kitbag with a wave to the motorist who had given me a lift from Bromley Station, a klaxon sounded and from tannoy loudspeakers by the gate a voice said, 'Seventy-two Squadron, scramble! scramble! Sixty-six to readiness!'

A big RAF policeman wearing a tin hat stood at the side of the entrance, gazing somewhat anxiously skywards. Proffering my bits of paper I said, 'AC 2 Mullins posted to Sixty-six Squadron, Corporal.' He took my papers and glanced at them out the corner of his eye. He seemed more interested in the sky than he was in me.

'Report to the orderly room on the left here,' he said, pushing the papers back at me. And as I picked up my kitbag again and moved away he shouted, 'And if that siren goes you jump down the nearest hole, got that, Airman?'

I turned and nodded. 'Yes Corporal.'

He started to say something else but whatever it was was lost in the roar of engines as six Spitfires ripped by close overhead, almost nose to tail, wheels folding as they went.

In the orderly room a flight sergeant took my papers, glanced at them briefly, and said, 'I think you'd better start in the armoury, as an armourer's mate, in the morning. Haven't you got a steel helmet?'

'Yes, Flight Sergeant.'

'Well wear it, that's what it was issued for.'

At Bridgnorth the only thing that could threaten my head was perhaps a skylark relieving himself; I hadn't thought of the steel helmet as anything more than a useless encumberance like the gas mask, but now I rummaged it out of the kitbag and put it on my head like the man said. He now addressed himself to an ordinary airman like myself who was sitting at a little desk in the corner.

'Thompson, take this airman to the stores and get him some bedding, and find him a space somewhere with Sixty-six Squadron.'

'Yes, Flight.' He rose with a sigh and picked up his helmet and gas mask. 'Let's go.'

As I followed him out of the building a long bonnet sports car almost entirely covered in young men wearing flying jackets hurtled through the gate almost running us down, and disappeared in the direction of the aerodrome.

'Them's your bloody pilots,' growled my guide, 'daft bastards, they'll kill somebody one day.'

From the stores we collected an empty palliasse and three blankets, and proceeded to a tin hut inside of which was a load of straw. He pointed to the straw. 'Make this do for now, you'll probably get some biscuits later.' He flipped open the mouth of the palliasse. 'Take as much as you like,' he said, 'There's plenty of it.'

I said, 'Christ it's back to the old donkey's breakfast!'

He smiled. 'I suppose that's what it is,' he said, 'a

146

donkey's breakfast, that's a funny expression, where d'you get that?'

I said, 'A long time ago brother, another time, another place.'

When we'd filled the palliasse and gone outside, he said, 'Wait here a minute.'

An RAF fifteen hundredweight van came round the corner. My guide put his hand up and it came to a stop. The driver put his head out, 'What's up?'

'You've got to take this bloke and his kit down the Church Hall.'

'Who said so?'

'Flight Sergeant Watkins.'

'Sod Flight Sergeant Watkins.'

My friend was already stuffing my gear into the back of the truck. And I jumped in behind it.

'You're a bleedin' nuisance,' shouted the driver at him as we drove away.

'Ah stop binding, get some in!'

'And you.'

The Church Hall was a sea of mattresses and bedding equipment, round the walls and up the centre. Here and there men were talking, laughing, playing cards, shouting, sleeping, writing home.

'Hey Sprog, where you from?'

'Bridgnorth.'

'You should have stayed there, there's sod all here.'

'Stop binding Johnson, you know you love it.'

'What's your name, mate?'

'Spike, Spike Mullins.'

'Put your bed down here Spike, next to mine, plenty of room here.'

'Watch him Spike, he's after pinching your boots, because he's got none to go on leave in.'

'I'm going to the cookhouse, who's coming? Come on Sprog, we'll show you where the cookhouse is.'

They don mufflers and greatcoats, some wear forage caps and some battered tin helmets, one or two with a squadron crest on the front. I can see now why they know I'm a sprog. My greatcoat is blue with shiny buttons, theirs are grey with buttons dull or missing. One has a rent stitched up with copper wire. My shiny black boots contrast ridiculously with their muddy turned down pirate style wellingtons. But there's not much I can do about it until I've 'got some in'. I march beside them as they slouch with an almost deliberate indifference up the lane in the gathering winter dusk. Another group meets us going in the opposite direction.

'Seventy-six just lost another kite. Shot up over Canterbury. Tried to land, went straight into the runway from fifty feet – Ching!'

I didn't know they went, 'Ching!'

'Bits of pilot all over the place.'

'His own fault, shouldn't have joined if he can't take a joke. What's for tea?'

'Sausage and chips.'

'What again!?'

We file through a well-worn gap in the hedge.

'Watch out for bomb holes, they're everywhere.'

We step across the strewn sandbags of what must have been a circular gun emplacement and down a path, through a doorway, past the blackout curtain into the dining room. Lines of trestle tables with men eating and talking. As we line up at the counter a voice behind us barks, 'Orderly officer! Any complaints?' I spring to attention, nobody else seems to take any notice. A young officer in Irvin jacket and

148

flying boots accompanied by a sergeant approaches the counter where we stand. He addresses one of my companions.

'Grub all right, Johnson?'

'Don't know sir, we haven't had any yet sir.'

The officer studies Johnson and the other two for a moment, with some distaste.

'You three,' he says at last, 'have got to be the three scruffiest erks on the squadron, you look like the last remnants of the bloody Polish Army.'

'Can't help it sir, lost all our gear at West Malling.'

'Don't give me that bullshit, Smith, I bet you three were in full flight, with all your worldly goods, before the Hun ever got to us, weren't you?'

'Yessir.'

'It's him sir,' one of them points at me, 'we look all right when he's not near us.'

'Piss off.'

'Yessir.'

Suddenly as I penned those last few words a little voice inside me said, 'Oh God, not another ratmalian rotten war story!'

'Hush! Hush!' I chided. 'Kindly don't interrupt the writer.'

'Hush! Hush! yourself, you foureyed fool,' it replied. 'It's all been done mate, four thousand books have been written, many by people who were actually there.'

'I was there.'

'So what? Big deal! Who cares?'

'I care.'

'All right, leave what you've already written to satisfy your little ego, mate.'

'What about those few who still like war stories?'

149

'Give 'em a quick condensed version of the rugged violence, not forgetting the romantic angle.'

'All right.'

'Bang, bang Charlie you're dead.'

'Bang, bang lady you're done.'

'You're a genius.'

'Thank you.'

I left the RAF in 1945 with, to my way of thinking, all the clothes and money that anybody could possibly need, £200 and a new suit, and took lodgings in Eltham in South East London. Soon I was the toast of the King's Head. I not only gave away money to people with hard luck stories, I gave money to people with good luck stories. I lived on beer and the finest fish and chips that money could buy. Days were spent in the cloistered tranquillity of the snooker hall above Burton the tailor's. The evenings were a frantic whirl of nonstop gaiety, pausing only to make love or throw up, not necessarily in that order.

Once, blinded by infatuation for a girl who said she could only return my affections if I went to work every day like her father did, I took a job as a labourer to a local builder. On my first morning he sent me off with some building materials on a handcart to a site about twenty minutes' walk away. On the way to the site I dropped in at Burton's for a quick couple of frames of snooker. And on my way back who should I bump into but a chap called Ginger Dobson who used to be in the RAF with me?

After a couple or three pints in the King's Head and a little chat about old times, Ginger said he'd better be getting home because he was married now. So, as he was going my way, I offered him a lift on my handcart which he accepted. When we got to the builder's yard the builder was standing at the gate making little jerky movements and strange noises. I tried to explain to him about bumping into my old comrade Ginger, and attempted an introduction, but he didn't seem to want to know and gave me my cards, which he happened to have in his hand at the time. As there seemed nothing else to do I went home with Ginger, whose wife didn't seem too thrilled to see me either.

When I related the adventures of the day to my loved one in the King's Head that evening, she laughed merrily until I got to the bit where I got the sack, then her ruby lips took on the aspect of a half healed razor slash, and, smartly finishing her gin and orange, she headed for the door and out of my life for ever. An experience that told me I was not yet ready for either marriage or general labouring. So, on with the ball!

But alas the ball was nearly over; it ended soon after I became a partner in the purchase of about a hundred stolen ladies' powder compacts. My partner in the enterprise was one Benny Isaacs, a doorway tout for various East End gentlemen's outfitters, who often boasted that he had once for a bet charmed a man off a bus in Aldgate High Street and into a shop where he bought a suit that he didn't want.

The ladies' compacts were pretty things made of real plastic. And as such fripperies were in short supply at the time we had no trouble in selling them around the local pubs and clubs and snooker halls.

Our downfall came about because Benny, who was doing the actual vending, had such a gift of the gab that he was getting very inflated prices, as much as a pound a time for something that cost us about two shillings and was worth maybe about five shillings.

151

The picture on the lid became 'an original daguerreotype motif that carries our personal warranty of authenticity.' 'The mirror is sealed and silvered on its reverse and will last a lifetime.' The bit of brass work inside the compact became 'electrolite geranium, a new invention proven for its harmless properties to ladies' delicate skins.'

By Saturday night of that week we had sold them all, and our pockets did jingle. That Sunday morning, according to custom, I left my lodgings at about half past eleven to stroll down to the King's Head, where I would perch on the cemetery wall opposite, in company with others of the drinking fraternity, and watch the world go by until the publican opened his doors at twelve o'clock to let us in. Passing Woolworth with plenty of time to spare, I lingered to admire a pair of young ladies dressing the front window, when to my horror I noticed that a part of the window they had already dressed contained ladies' compacts, our compacts, hundreds of them, marked, 'five shillings each'. A voice behind me said, 'You've seen 'em then?' It was Benny Isaacs.

I nodded because I didn't know what to say. There was hardly a villain or a publican in the area who hadn't paid two, three, or even four times the shop value for one of these articles in the last few days.

'Some people round here are going to be very annoyed with us,' he continued. 'Some people are going to want to cut our ears off, ain't they my boy?'

Even in my condition of acute distress I couldn't help looking at his own ears which stuck out like pink jug handles, and wondering if his black velour Anthony Eden trilby would fall down over his eyes without them. I must have smiled involuntarily at the image the thought conjured up in my mind.

'It's not funny, Spike,' he said, shaking his head dolefully. 'Not funny at all, there are some very uncivilized people about, very uncivilized indeed. What are you going to do?'

I said, 'I think I'd better leave town for a while, that's what I'll do.'

He thought for a moment. 'That's a very good idea,' he said, 'a very good idea. Then I can put it about that I was only working for you and you've got all the money and gone off with it, which makes me one of the injured parties, don't it?' He was almost jubilant.

'Wait a minute,' I said, 'I don't want my name bandied about town as if I'm a thief or something.'

He shrugged and spread his palms in the characteristic gesture of his race. 'What else can you do?' he asked. 'What else can you do?' He turned to go. 'Now take care of yourself, won't you my boy?' And he strode off jauntily down Eltham High Street in the direction of the King's Head.

CHAPTER 10

My sister with whom I had kept in touch during the war – she used to drive her ARP ambulance into Biggin Hill and take a load of us up the pub for a drink sometimes – now lived in Pimlico where she found me a two-roomed flat over a burnt out shop behind Victoria Station. The flat consisted of a front bedroom overlooking Warwick Way, and a kitchen at the back overlooking a brick wall. It was nominally a furnished flat but the previous tenants had apparently grown so fond of the furniture that when they left they had taken most of it with them, including the linoleum, leaving a kitchen table and two kitchen chairs, a gas stove, and some saucepans. There was also a high backed wickerwork armchair that was so full of woodworm that I swear you could hear the denizens eating it while you were sitting in it.

The landlord, who was Polish, explained to me, mostly in Polish, that while he had no intention of bankrupting himself buying even more furniture for the place he would see to it that I got a bed to sleep in. Then he went off, to reappear some time later carrying an iron framed camp bed and a mattress bearing a label saying, 'A gift from the Canadian Red Cross.' Unfortunately it was a child's bed, and as I am about a foot and a half taller than the average child I had to make up the difference, to save my feet sticking out into space, with an empty orange box at the foot of the

154

bed covered by the cushion off the wicker chair, and take great care not to kick out during the night or it all fell over and I had to make it all up again.

I had never in my life had a place really to call my own before and I loved it. The first week I spent Darkalining the floors and cleaning the windows and cooking such delicacies as fried egg sandwich and fried eggs on toast and fried eggs. And when the egg ration ran out I made dried egg sandwiches. However, whether I liked it or not, I was not to be alone for very long.

One early evening I left the door ajar when I popped over to the corner delicatessen for a meat pie for tea and returned to find I had a visitor. The visitor was a great ginger tomcat who sat on the wicker chair in the kitchen washing himself. He paused and looked at me and continued his ablutions. Reopening the door behind me, I said, 'Puss, puss, come on, on your way.' He stopped licking and stared at me with unblinking great greeny eyes and settled himself down in my chair as if he'd always been there.

When I saw 'Puss, good pussy' wasn't going to work, I marched over to him and said, 'Go on, piss off, out!' putting out my hand to give him a push in the right direction. But before I could touch him a lightning paw flashed and he'd opened my thumb clean as a razor, ears back, growling a deep-throated growl like a dog. I didn't know cats growled, it frightened the life out of me. Now I was in a quandary. I couldn't bring myself to hit him, although he didn't have many scruples about hurting me. I could chuck some water over him but that would make my cushion all wet, and now I could see he was thin and gaunt under all that fur, and it didn't seem right to make him wet and miserable, evil as he was. This was something that needed thinking about. He watched me as I fried some chips to go with my pie. The thought occurred to me that perhaps if I gave him something to eat he might be in a better mood to go back to the bomb site where he probably came from. I put it to him straight while I opened a tin of meat and veg out of my stock in the cupboard.

'Cat,' I said, 'I'm going to give you some grub, and then it's goodnight, hit the breeze, OK?'

He slurped down half a tin of meat and veg in about ten seconds then jumped back on the chair and growled at me when I took the empty plate away. Then I gave him some sterilized milk, but he didn't like that so I tried some water; that was OK.

After tea I lit the fire and he left his chair and curled up in front of it. I said, 'Don't make yourself too comfortable, cat, it's the great outdoors for you, and if you give me a hard time you'll feel the toe of my boot up your backside.' When I looked out of the bedroom window it was dark and murky with a few snowflakes falling. The street girls who paraded their wares opposite were stamping their feet and hugging their coats around them. I went back to the kitchen and he opened one eye and looked at me. I said, 'I can't chuck you out in that, cat, even the whores are freezing, tomorrow morning, right?' It suddenly struck me for a moment as a bit ludicrous that I was talking to a cat, but I used to have conversations with the mice under our kitchen range at home so why shouldn't I talk to a cat?

After I'd washed up I sat down in front of the fire with my shoes off reading a book and he started purring. Then I thought, it's rather nice to have another living thing around, perhaps I'll let him stay, if he behaves himself and gets a bit more sociable. No sooner had I thought these kind thoughts than my sockinged foot must have brushed against him, and he had me by the big toe with his front claws and was all set to bite it off if I hadn't clouted him with a handy shoe.

'Right,' I snarled, limping over to the cupboard that contained my little medicine box. 'Right, you ungrateful bastard, out you go in the morning. I'm not spending my life covered in bloody iodine just for you, you can bloody well freeze for all I care.'

The next morning when I awoke the cat was standing at the door waiting for me to let him out, and when I did he disappeared in the direction of the bomb site across the road. But when I returned from getting some shopping and books from the library he was sitting on the doorstep and bounded up the stairs as soon as I opened the door as if the place belonged to him, which apparently he had decided it did. Within a week he had stopped growling at me and the time came when, while I was reading in front of the fire, he climbed on to the arm of my chair and thence warily on to my lap. I don't know when I felt so privileged, as I sat carefully turning the pages of my book, so as not to frighten him into running away or attacking me.

That night he decided to confer further honour upon me by sleeping at the foot of the bed on my feet. The cat had put a lot of weight on since moving in and, try as I could, I found it impossible to sleep with him lying across my feet. Eventually I sleepily sat up and, reaching down to the foot of the bed, I said, 'It's no use, you'll have to get off.' A rapier claw tore the top of my waving finger in the darkness.

157

'You bloody sod,' I roared, 'get off!' and kicked out from beneath the blankets. The orange box supporting the cushion turned over and the end of the bed fell off. It was a bitterly cold night so I lay in the foetal position in what was left of the bed, fighting against the logic that sooner or later I would have to get out and make it again, and put something on my bleeding finger.

When I eventually put the light on, the cat was sitting upright, motionless, in the corner of the room, his back to me, looking at the wallpaper. Muttering and shivering I made the bed again and put some iodine and a piece of old shirt on my finger. When I got back into bed again I couldn't sleep. I could feel his presence in the corner of the room, all alone on my bare Darkaline floor boards. I knew he was thinking, and that he was thinking about me. And it's not nice to have someone sitting in the corner of a dark room thinking about you.

Now if I strained my eyes I could see his shadowy outline in the glimmer from the street lights through the curtains. To hell with him, what's he got to sulk about, two meals a day, which is more than I often get? If it wasn't for me he would be out there in the snow on the bomb site with his friends.

'Puss! Come on cat, come on puss, it's all right mate.' The shadow in the corner never moved, I somehow knew he wouldn't. When I picked him up and put him back on the end of the bed he neither resisted nor cooperated. But when I pushed my feet carefully down in the space that was left to me he started purring and I knew we were friends again.

Jobs were very scarce, especially for an ex-leading aircraftman armourer with not much more to offer than five years' experience with bombs, machine guns and small arms, knowledge that had suddenly become about as useful as an ashtray on a motorbike. The only worthwhile legacy of my time in the RAF was that, to offset the boredom of the barrack-room, I had over the years developed an insatiable appetite for books and a love of the written word. Once, urged on by friends who had read little stories and articles I had written, I even joined an English class on the base to learn how to become a writer. But instead of revealing to me how I could become a Thurber or a Steinbeck or a Saroyan in three easy lessons, the first week was spent by the teacher explaining the construction of a sentence and the usage of verbs, nouns, pronouns, and so on. To this day I have really no idea what he was talking about, and I left at the end of the week just as bewildered as I had begun. So that while I still continued to do some writing, the possibility of making any money out of it seemed rather remote, although I had a feeling that it could be done.

The cat and I got very hungry that winter. Often we had cornflakes for breakfast, cornflakes for dinner and cornflakes for tea, with a break at weekends when the dole money came in when we had a blowout on dried egg and bacon and tins of meat and veg and spam.

'Herrings,' said the *Daily Mirror*, 'herrings are at this moment the cheapest, most nourishing items that anybody could wish for, they are packed with fat, protein and vitamins.'

'Cat,' I said, 'this is just what we need to build us up big and strong again, don't go away I'll be right back.' So, taking the shilling that I had been saving for a rainy day off the mantelpiece, I went out to return with two of the fattest, most protein-filled, vitamin conscious herrings that money could buy. When I cooked them we had one each. Then when we'd finished he threw up in the corner and I threw up in the sink. Apparently our bodies weren't quite ready for such richness all in one go, not just yet.

Of course, at that time, the cat and I were by no means the only ones feeling the pinch; almost every newspaper and magazine carried recipes for concocting good satisfying dishes without resorting to cannibalism.

'How to prepare the label off a tin of pilchards for a family of six.'

'Carrot trifle for four.'

'Garbage Surprise.'

'How to flavour a chair leg.'

I'm sure that if someone had announced the nutritional value of snow, the streets would have been cleared in no time.

It was from one of these sources that I got the idea of stewing marrowbones to produce 'lots of rich marrowbone dripping and rich marrowbone jelly.' 'Marrowbones,' it said, 'are easily obtainable from your friendly neighbourhood butcher.' Friendly butchers being about as plentiful that winter as butterflies, it was some time before I eventually marched home with my parcel of bones; in fact I'd almost gone off the idea, which, as it turned out, would have been just as well.

The pieces of bone were all about twice as long as my largest saucepan was deep. I tried shortening one of them by placing one end of the bone on the raised tiles of the hearth surround and giving it a terrific clout in the middle with the poker, but all that happened was that some of the tiles shattered, and the cat

160

Mary.

who was asleep at the time nearly made a hole in the door. The bones, or submerged parts of them, simmered happily away, filling the flat with the aroma of boiled bones, until it was time for bed when I turned the gas off to allow the rich marrowbone jelly and dripping to set on the surface ready to be put in jars and basins on the morrow.

Come the dawn, I said, 'Cat, what's it going to be for breakfast? Fried bread? Dripping toast? Bread and dripping? Perhaps a saucer of rich marrowbone jelly?' The surface of the water when we looked was covered in a thin grey scum, about a sixteenth of an inch thick with a consistency of thin ice. And an exploration of the bottom revealed nothing more than you might find in the U bend of an average sink. It was with a heavy heart that I reversed the bones so that the ends that had been sticking out all night were now submerged, and lit the gas again.

By day three the scum was beginning to look a bit more promising but the bones were taking on a greyish colour like bones that had seen better days. On day four I unexpectedly got a day's work for Bishops the removal people, carrying furniture from a deserted church where it had been stored during the war, and when I got home the water had almost boiled away leaving a brown slurping residue covering the bottom of the pan, which with the grey bleached bones sticking out looked and smelt not unlike a tiny area of some bubbling primeval swamp where mammoths go to die. That night I tossed the whole lot out of the front window hoping they might start a murder investigation during which I would send the police anonymous letters saying, 'The butcher did it.'

The chef's office, in the depths of the Grosvenor

Hotel, Victoria, was warm and cosy as the womb after the bitter cold of the icebound streets outside. I stood the other side of the desk from the bulky figure swathed in starched and spotless linen for perhaps four or five minutes before he stopped writing, put down his fountain pen, and, leaning back in his chair, took a long dispassionate look at me.

The commissionaire on the front door, from whom I'd enquired if there were any jobs going in the hotel, had told me the chef was an 'Itie' to which I'd replied that I didn't care if he was a Nazi as long as he gave me a job. The chef took a gulp of the wine from the glass in front of him, wiped his big black moustache on the corner of the napkin round his throat, and relit a half burnt cigar from the ashtray before he spoke.

'It is very cold outside.'

'Yes,' I replied, 'it's colder than yesterday, they say there's more snow on the . . .'

He interrupted me with a wave of the cigar. 'Have you come here to work, or to get out of the cold?'

The newsreel pictures I had seen of thousands of ragged, abject, defeated Italians flashed before my eyes. Broken they were, practically begging for mercy. And here, almost before they'd been counted, was one of them, fat, sleek and oily, wine in one hand, cigar in the other, addressing me as if I'd lost the war not him. There is a limit to which British pride can be pushed, but fortunately I had not reached that limit yet.

'I've come to work.'

'Hm, you any good at washing pots and pans?'

'I'm ultrasensational.'

'What you saying?'

'I'm very good.'

162

'Come.'

He rose and waddled out of the door and I followed him across the appetizing hubbub of the kitchens to a room with great galvanized iron sinks at which a man in shirtsleeves and wearing a black rubber apron was washing saucepans.

'Hey Jan,' called the chef, 'look, I've got somebody to help you!'

The man at the sink turned and nodded without any great show of enthusiasm. He was about middle aged and stockily built, his hair close-cropped to his scalp and his features melancholy and lined.

'This is Jan,' said the chef, putting a friendly arm around the shoulders of the other man. 'Jan is from Poland, he does not say very much, but he is a good man. You are a good man, eh Jan?'

The man smiled slightly and nodded.

'You find apron for this man.'

Jan reached behind the door and handed me a rubber apron, and as he did so I noticed a number tattooed on the inside of his forearm. So Jan was from a concentration camp.

When the chef had gone, I said, 'Well Jan, here we are, I'm Spike, Spike Mullins, where do we start?'

Nudging some saucepans on the floor, with his boot, he pointed to the sink. 'You wash,' he said, 'I fetch,' and wandered off into the kitchens, returning a few minutes later bearing some more dirty utensils which he dropped on top of the others.

'You want food?' he asked quietly, pointing a finger at his mouth.

I said, 'As a matter of fact I could do with a snack mate, yes I want food.'

He laid a stubby finger across his lips and looked

163

round furtively as he dipped into the large pocket across the front of his rubber apron and produced the best part of a kipper which he placed on the draining area of the sink in front of me. Then diving back in, he brought forth two sausages and the rest of the kipper which he also put on the draining board, and with greasy hands pushed towards me. For a moment I thought it was a joke. It used to be thought funny among my friends in the RAF to 'accidentally' drop a piece of bread and jam on the floor, jam side down, and then proceed with great pains to clean it up to eat for the revulsion of any uninitiated strangers that were watching.

'Good,' he said, with more furtive glances. Almost lost for something to say upon realizing that he was seriously making me a gift of the repulsive little pile, I said, 'Yes thank you, thank you very much.'

'More?'

'No thanks, er, this'll do me fine.'

He laid a warning finger across his lips again and sidled off into the kitchen. As he left, one of the younger cooks came whistling in. 'Hello mate,' he said. 'Just started? Got a clean strainer for me?' The little pile of sausages and kipper remnants on the draining board caught his eye, and he started to laugh. 'Old Jan's got you at it, has he?' I had to laugh myself. 'I'm supposed to eat that,' I said.

'I know,' he chuckled, 'he still thinks we're all in the bleedin' concentration camp. It's our only entertainment out there, watching him sliding round pinching bits of grub off the range, you'd be amazed what goes into that pocket of his. Poor sod.'

I said, 'What am I supposed to do with it? I'm not *that* hungry.'

He said, 'Chuck it in the bin when he's not looking. Don't want to hurt his feelings. When you want something to eat come and see me, I'll see you all right.'

Every morning of the two months that I worked in that kitchen at the Grosvenor, Jan brought me something to eat. Sometimes a few bits of bacon, cooked or raw, or perhaps a handful of devilled kidneys. Fried eggs were the most repulsive, because once an egg has been fried it does not travel well, to say the least, especially in the pocket of a greasy rubber apron. When he caught me wrapping up a few of the items in a piece of newspaper, to take home to the cat, he looked very suspicious. 'What you do?' he grunted. I said, 'I'm taking it home for my wife.' I thought he might get shirty if I said I was giving the food to an animal.

And once, when a girl from the office upstairs came down to ask me something about my insurance cards while I happened to be making up a little parcel of haddock and meat pie mixture, Jan said, 'Is for his wife.' She looked a bit startled, but said nothing. God knows what stories were told about me around the upper echelons of the Grosvenor Hotel.

CHAPTER 11

I left the Grosvenor Hotel without any great regrets soon after I made contact with Vic Oliver. Vic Oliver was one of the leading comedians of the day at that period, a star of stage and radio. His speciality was a solo act with a violin or a piano, during which he told jokes about the musical instrument or the racehorses that he owned. He would peer into the fret holes of the violin and say, 'This is a very old instrument. I'm not sure whether this is the date in here, sixteen hundred and nine, or the price, sixteen and ninepence.' He would play a wrong note and say, 'Excuse me, I haven't had much practice, it's been so cold outdoors lately.' Then he would cough and turn up the collar of his immaculate dinner jacket, and say, 'I must get a room tonight.'

Talking of his horses, he would say, 'I wouldn't back it to win, on its present form I wouldn't even back it to live.'

'I said to my horse, "The way you've been running you ought to be pulling a milk cart." He said, "And the way you're playing you ought to be driving it." '

He was a sort of English equivalent of Jack Benny or Victor Borge.

So it was one evening while listening to Vic Oliver on the old radio I'd bought that the thought occurred to me that perhaps I could write the sort of things he was saying. For the next couple of days I thought

166

about nothing but what could be said that would make people laugh about violins, pianos, and racehorses.

'I'm now going to play Beethoven's fourth piano concerto, the second movement, opus five, in C sharp minor, and I'd like you all to join in the chorus.'

'I took my string of racehorses to Ascot and the string broke and they all fell down.'

'I was going to play something of Brahms, but why should I? He never plays anything of mine.'

These were the sort of gags I wrote, which may not seem so funny now, and perhaps weren't so funny then either.

When I had assembled two or three foolscap sheets of the above I posted them with a little letter which was practically an apology for being alive and having the temerity to think I could write gags, and posted them to:

Mr Victor Oliver,
c/o The BBC,
Broadcasting House,
London.

He was known to the listening millions as 'Vic Oliver' but I felt that to actually write that on an envelope might be taken as familiarity and put him off me before I'd started. For the next few mornings I hung around outside the front door when the post-man was due, in case the letter-box developed some technical fault and threw letters out again, or the postman had forgotten that people still lived here and wanted reminding. Eventually my patience was rewarded with the most exciting letter I'd ever had in my life.

Dear Mr Mullins,
Thank you for sending me the jokes. You obvi-
ously have a real talent for humorous writing
and I would like to see some more of your work.
In the meantime I will pay you half a guinea a
joke, the same as my other writers, for every one
of yours that I use after I have tried them out, if
that is agreeable to you.

Kindest regards,
Vic Oliver.

Suddenly I'm a writer! A talented writer! This man,
star of stars, talker on the wireless, a divine being, has
said so, right there on paper, in real typing!

Dear Mr Oliver,
Thank you for your letter. I will be very pleased
if you would be good enough to use any of the
gags I sent you on the terms you have mentioned.
Thank you again,

Yours sincerely,
Spike Mullins.

Dear Mr Mullins,
I am going to try out some of your gags on my
radio show this coming Sunday evening. And
will let you know how they go.

Kindest regards,
Vic Oliver.

That Sunday I enjoyed for the first time the inde-
scribable feeling of hearing people actually laughing
at something that I had actually written down, out of

my own head, on a piece of paper. Something that had never been heard in the whole world before I thought of it.

Dear Mr Mullins,
Please find enclosed postal orders to the value of £2-2-0 for 'the string broke', 'play something by Brahms', 'all join in the chorus', and the 'piano' gag.
These all went very well, and I am looking forward to seeing some more of your work quite soon.

Kindest regards,
Vic Oliver.

But there were six of them, I heard them myself. What about 'my horse was unlucky in the Grand National, he fell just before the first jump'? And, 'now I'd like to sing you Musetta's waltz song from *La Bohème* by Puccini, but unfortunately I don't know the words'? They must have been the two that didn't get much of a laugh. Of course, no laugh no money. That's what he must have meant by 'trying them out'.

Ah well, at least I'd cracked it, I could turn bits of paper out of a kid's exercise book into money!

'Excuse me milkman, could you cash this postal order for me? One of those Vic Oliver sent me this morning.'

What a grand life it was going to be! I'd get a night job so that I could write all day and work at night until I'd be making so much money from writing that I wouldn't have to go to work anymore. Then I'd buy a silk cravat and a velvet smoking jacket and I'd go and take my place among all the actors and writers and beautiful people in the pubs over Chelsea way.

By the time I found a job in an all night café near Waterloo Bridge things weren't going too well with Mr Oliver. Out of ten gags I'd send him, he would, on average, use five and pay me for three. And I was getting a bit depressed about the whole thing. As a writer earning about thirty-one shillings and sixpence a week it would be a long time before I became the toast of the Chelsea set.

I didn't like the night job in the café near Waterloo Bridge. I didn't like the crotchety old fool who shared the nightshift with me. I didn't like serving the spivs and thugs who frequented the place till the early hours. And I resented the poor shaky night drifters who fell asleep on the stools round the walls with their heads on the shelf among the teacups, because I had to wake them, and say, 'I'm sorry you can't sleep here, you'll have to go somewhere else,' and know how they hated me for bringing them back from their little holiday from life.

I'd only been working in the café a few nights, when:

Dear Mr Mullins,
Perhaps you would like to drop in and see me about eight o'clock some evening in my dressing room at the London Casino so that we can have a little chat about things.

Kindest regards,
Vic Oliver.

This is it! The big time! Strike while the iron is hot! Tonight's the night! Make hay while the sun shines!

170

Most of the day I spent cleaning my only suit with a bottle of petrol I'd got from the garage for twopence. 'I wonder if you could oblige me with a drop of petrol in my bottle. Got a couple of spots on the suit and I'm meeting Vic Oliver tonight at the London Casino.'

Seven o'clock found me briskly striding along Victoria Street in the direction of the London Casino in a personal cloud of petrol fumes. I hope it doesn't rain, I haven't got a coat or the fare for the bus, and if I turn up all wet he'll probably refuse to see me. Perhaps he's going to give me a job as his personal writer. Bob Hope has personal writers, why shouldn't Vic Oliver? Perhaps he's going to get me a job at the BBC. I'd like that.

'I'm a writer with the BBC.' That sounds very important, that does. That will roll off the tongue – frequently.

Finishing the last of my three Woodbines that I'd been saving to smoke when I needed them, during the interview, I made a bolt for the stage door of the London Casino dead on eight o'clock.

'Mr Mullins, Spike Mullins, to see Mr Oliver.'

The stage doorkeeper disappeared out of his box without comment returning a few moments later with a young, rather effeminate young man.

'Mr Mullins?'

'Yes.'

'Will you come this way? I'm Graham, Mr Oliver's manager and general factotum.'

'Oh, pleased to meet you.'

'Yes.'

He knocked on a door, 'Mr Mullins, Mr Oliver!'

'Come in.'

I'd seen Vic Oliver on stage a couple of weeks

previously from the 'gods' at the Golders Green Empire. This man in a dressing gown with his bare legs sticking out and make-up on his face looked smaller and older. He shook my hand warmly and there was no mistaking the American-Austrian intonation of the voice when he said, 'Mr Mullins, it's so nice to meet you at last. Come and sit down, did you have a good journey?' I nodded. 'Yes, thank you Mr Oliver.'

He moved a violin in its case from a chair for me and I wondered fleetingly whether it smelt the same as mine had done.

'Do you smoke?' he asked, proffering a gold cigarette case. 'They are Camels, American cigarettes I'm afraid. Do you like American cigarettes?'

I said, 'Yes, I smoked them a lot when I was with the American Air Force occasionally during the war.'

I don't know why I troubled to tell him that, perhaps I hoped he'd give me a packet. Or perhaps he'd think, 'Here is one of the guys who did his bit when the chips were down, I must look after him.' As it turned out I would be wrong on both counts.

'Have you brought me some jokes to look at?'

I handed him a couple of sheets of writing that I'd been intending to post. He read the words silently, his face creasing to a smile two or three times.

'Very good,' he said at last, 'very good, there are quite a few lines in there that I'll try out as soon as I get an opportunity. What do you do for a living, Mr Mullins?' Here it comes, opportunity is knocking Spike.

'I work in an all night café, Mr Oliver, but I was sort of wondering whether I could get a regular job in this business.'

172

'Doing what?' His friendly blue eyes had lost some of their sparkle.

Deep breath. 'As a writer perhaps.'

He shook his head slowly, 'I don't know anyone who employs his own writers on a permanent basis, and I certainly couldn't afford to.'

'Perhaps I could get a job at the BBC?'

'You never know, why not drop them a line and find out?'

Someone rapped on the door and called, 'Five minutes, Mr Oliver!' He rose to his feet and held out his hand, 'Well thank you for coming Mr Mullins, keep up the good work. Goodbye.'

Sad and bewildered I made my way through the jostling West End crowds towards Waterloo. Half an hour ago I was a writer with his feet on the ladder of success, now I was a nothing with his feet on the pavement taking him to work in a stinking café the same as last night. The only consolation was that as soon as I got behind the counter I would be able to pinch myself twenty Woodbines off the shelf and a couple of shillings out of the till as I'd done every night. At least I'd have a smoke and be slightly solvent again.

When I entered the café the fat middle-aged man who had engaged me for the job at head office was standing at the counter talking to the old fool that I worked with.

'Oh, so you've arrived,' sneered Fatty. 'Eight o'clock is your time, in case you'd forgotten.'

I said, 'I'm sorry, I got held up. I'll get my apron and make a start.'

My erstwhile colleague put out his hand to stop me lifting the flap to pass behind the counter.

'No you don't,' he crowed. 'I've told the guv'nor here about you nicking those fags off the shelf last night. I saw you.'

The other man said, 'What do you think we're running here, a charity? Turn up when you like and help yourself? No my friend, you are sacked. Goodnight.'

I said. 'That's all right, where's my wages?'

'Call in the office Monday,' he answered, 'now, hoppit!'

If it wasn't my night, it wasn't his either. He wasn't to know he was talking to a man who had observed his whole future, complete with silk cravat and velvet smoking jacket, destroyed with a few nonchalant words within the last hour.

Trying hard to keep my voice steady enough to make sense, I said, 'Listen, you ponce, I've had a very bad day, and if things get any worse I'm going to kill somebody, and it'll probably be you and this bloody old nanny goat behind you. Now give me my money.' I held out my hand.

The fool behind the counter squeaked, 'Shall I go and get a policeman?' And nobody answered him.

My employer straightened himself up. 'Now that's no way to go talking to people . . . .' He stopped, sensing that I probably meant what I'd said, pulled a fat notecase from his back pocket and looking sheepishly around at the customers who were now watching with interest, extracted three pound notes and put them in my hand.

'That's all I can let you have right now,' he growled; 'if you had asked properly you could have had it without all this goings on.'

When I got near the door his friend behind the

counter shouted, 'And don't come back in here again or we'll get the police to you!'

I stopped, picked up an empty bottle off one of the tables and made as though to throw it, and he ducked sideways with such vigour that he nearly knocked himself out on the frame of the door behind him. I had thought that I'd never laugh again but I couldn't help it then.

CHAPTER 12

Soon it was summertime and the living was easy. London was being rebuilt and labouring work on building sites plentiful. My landlord stopped shouting through the letter-box for his rent or jumping out at me from shop doorways. The cat sunned himself all day on the wall surrounding the bomb site opposite, and waited for me to come home with his dinner and perhaps a few bottles of beer. The cat liked a drop of beer almost as much as I did. Although, after his second saucer, he invariably developed a tendency to fall off things and attack chairs and walls and other inanimate objects.

Flushed with the memory of my slight success with Mr Oliver, I wrote almost constantly, whenever I was not at work or asleep, jokes, sketches and stories. The sketches and jokes I sent to various comedians of the day, who in many cases didn't even answer, and in others sent them back with a little 'Thank you for your interest' note, the stories receiving just as short shrift from the publishers they visited. Once I retraced my steps in the direction of Vic Oliver but he had set off on a world tour and wouldn't return for a long time hence.

Perhaps, it occurred to me one day, perhaps I'm writing the wrong things, perhaps I should be writing something else. But what else is there? Seed catalogues? Cook books? Bedwetting for beginners?

Me with the 1978 Pye Colour Television Award finger print outfit.

Plays? That's it! I'll write a play. The West End theatres, I'd noticed, were full of plays by people I'd never even heard of: Terence Rattigan, Frederick Lonsdale, Emlyn Williams; if they could do it, then so could I. It then occurred to me that, while I had heard one or two plays on the wireless, I had never actually seen one, and it would do no harm to go along and have a quick glance at a play being performed in a West End theatre before replacing it with one of my own.

The evening found me seated in the gallery of the Apollo Theatre, Shaftesbury Avenue, watching a murder mystery entitled *Grand National Night* being performed by Hermione Baddeley, Leslie Banks and supporting cast. When the play was finished I had to admit to myself, somewhat reluctantly, that there did seem a bit more to this play-writing than met the eye. Perhaps if I got a job in the theatre and watched more plays then not only would the craft unfold itself to me but I would be on hand to show my play to the actors or the manager or whoever one shows plays to when they are written.

As I was leaving the theatre I spoke to the man downstairs who was waiting to shut the door. I said, 'How do I go about getting a job in a theatre, mate?'

'What sort of job?'

'Any job, I don't care.'

He said, 'Why don't you pop in and see the manager tomorrow? I think he wants someone to take over upstairs where you've just come from.'

The next evening I stood in the front of the gallery of the Apollo Theatre wearing a uniform cap, at least a size too big stuffed with newspaper, feeling very self important, looking down on the empty stage and the rows of empty red plush seats of the stalls.

From somewhere the muted strains of the *Eine Kleine Nachtmusik* start. The manager, an opulent figure in evening dress, strolls out on to the stage followed by a smaller figure in a blue uniform, the theatre fireman. They halt in the centre of the stage, and the usherettes' voices that have been calling and laughing from the upper circle below me are stilled. The manager looks up at me. 'All right in the gallery?' he calls.

It reminds me in a silly way of a lifeboat drill at sea. Wouldn't it be funny if I shouted, 'Number one boat ready, sir!' But I don't, I say, 'OK in the gallery, sir!' like the man told me to.

'All right upper circle?' he calls.

'OK sir!'

'Dress circle?'

'Yessir!'

'Stalls!'

'OK sir!'

'All right, let them in!'

By the time I take my place at the entrance to the gallery feet are running up the stone stairs. People come in two's and three's and four's. Excited, breathless from the climb. I tear their tickets and give them half.

'Let's sit here,' they say.

'No here, we'll see better from here.'

'What about over there?'

'Have you got any programmes?'

Christ, I've forgotten the programmes.

'Here you are sir, ninepence each.'

'That's a bit steep, ninepence, isn't it?'

178

'You're quite right sir, it's daylight robbery.'

'I say, Amanda, I told the chap the programmes were a bit pricey, and he said, "Quite right sir, it's daylight robbery."' Amanda is pretty, she turns and laughs at me. I think I might like this job.

I liked the theatre, even when it was empty and a bit shabby in the mornings when I helped to clean it, polishing the hundreds of ashtrays and brass handrails everywhere. I liked the theatre people, actors, actresses, dancers, when I saw them in the pubs and cafés, primping and preening, shouting, laughing, and forever showing off.

I can't recall how many times I saw *Grand National Night*. But I do know that in the end I had learned no more about writing plays than how to write *Grand National Night*. Strange as it may seem, one of the things I do have to thank the Apollo for is my introduction to the works of William Shakespeare, not however from the stage, but from the gutter outside. A speech from *Othello* recited nightly by a busker to the queue, wafting upwards through the window on the gallery landing. Each night he came, taking his turn with the man who sang 'Danny Boy', the lady with the accordion, and the man who played the spoons.

'Ladies and gentlemen,' he would begin in a commanding voice, 'Othello the Moor has married Desdemona! Her father is heartbroken that his fair daughter should marry a Moor, even Othello a gallant soldier in the service of his country. And he suspects witchcraft. And so Othello is brought before the Senate to defend himself with these wonderful words given to him by William Shakespeare.'

'Most potent, grave, and reverend signiors,' he says, 'My very noble and approved good masters, that

179

I have taken away this old man's daughter, It is most true; true, I have married her: The very head and front of my offending hath this extent, no more.' And on until, 'She loved me for the dangers I had passed, And I loved her that she did pity them. This only is the witchcraft I have used. Here comes the lady; let her witness it.'

Every evening I listened, until I could almost recite the words myself, as a would-be writer experiencing the same emotions that I had done when I'd once watched Joe Davis almost make the ultimate break and said to myself, 'Mullins, you should give up this game.'

But it passed.

It was while I was at the Apollo Theatre that I met Mary, the girl I was later to marry. I'd called at my sister's flat one Sunday evening and the front door was opened by a girl of about nineteen, dressed in not much more than a salmon pink silk dressing gown that, if it was meant to conceal anything, failed to conceal the fact that its owner was, as they say, stacked in all the right places, with at one end a pretty, smiling face, and at the other a pair of lovely long bare legs that didn't want to stay out of sight behind the dressing gown.

I said, 'I'm, er, I'm Spike, Kathleen's brother.'

She said, 'Yes I know, I've heard about you. I'm Mary, a friend of Kathleen's. Come on up.'

I didn't know my sister had friends like this! As I followed her up the stairs, so engrossed was I in the rippling rear view of the silk dressing gown that I fell over one of the stairs. I said, 'It's a bit dark on these stairs, isn't it? Could you hold my hand?'

She turned her head and flashed me a smile. 'No

180

thank you,' she replied. 'As I said, I've heard about you.'

'What have you heard?'

'It's been said that you're a bit – unpredictable?'

When we got inside my sister's flat, my sister introduced Mary as 'a friend staying here for the weekend.' And me as 'my brother, of whom less said the better.'

Later, when my sister's boyfriend turned up, we all went for a drink over Chelsea way. It was a warm summer evening, the pavements crowded with strolling people. When we'd had one drink and were leaving the pub to walk to the next one, I managed to let my sister and her bloke get a little way in front, then I grabbed Mary's lovely little hand and dragged her over to a nearby shop window.

'There's something here in this window I've been wanting to look at, d'you mind?' The shop I had unfortunately chosen in my panic to lose our companions was an undertaker's with nothing in the window but a few cremation urns and a black marble headstone. Before I could say, 'Oh, it must have changed hands since last week,' she said. 'This is a bit of luck, I didn't know this place was here. Let's go inside and have a look round. Come on, let's tell the man we're just browsing.'

I looked at this desirable bird with the long legs and the laughing eyes and the immaculate fashionable clothes and thought to myself, 'All that and a sense of humour, Mary, I think I'm going to like you.' And on her own confession, a lot later, she had said to herself, 'Spike Mullins, you're a rough diamond and you make me laugh, I think I'm going to marry you.'

We were married in Caxton Hall Registry Office about a year later. And her lovely Jewish mother, although I had still not written anything saleable, now referred to me as 'my son-in-law, the writer'. And her stern Scottish father, who could smell a waster a mile off, still referred to me as 'him'. The married condition really made no difference to our life style. We still ate together, laughed together, drank together, and slept together, as we had done almost since we met.

Mary still had her job in the offices of Littlewoods in Oxford Street and I was by now a porter in Dolphin Square, a complex of luxury flats just around the corner. Each Friday she pooled our wages and my tips, working out the weekly budget with most unjewish logic.

'That's two pounds for the rent, four pounds for food, we'll say three pounds for food. I hate gluttony, and the rest is for drink and debauchery and a taxi home. Where shall we go?'

'What about your fares next week?'

'I shall walk, it's good for my figure.'

'You said that last week, but you didn't.'

'Is it my fault it rained? Let's hit the wind.'

'The expression is – hit the breeze.'

'Breeze shmeeze, who cares? Let's go somewhere.'

We lived the life of Riley. Covent Garden for the Opera, Victoria Palace for the Crazy Gang, the Old Vic for Shakespeare. Supper to the Brasserie in Coventry Street. On nice evenings we went to the Eight Bells and Bowling Green pub in Chelsea and drank pints of bitter sitting on the kerb with our feet in the gutter, as was fashionable although very uncomfortable. When the mood took us we got up before dawn on Sunday mornings and wandered along the Thames Embankment to watch the sun come up over London, and have breakfast in Lyons' Corner House in the Strand. Sometimes we played truant from work and caught the Green Line bus to somewhere in the country and caught frogs and picked wild flowers and galloped about shouting, 'Isn't this marvellous!?'

It was at the end of one of these days in the country, when we were back home sitting outside the Eight Bells and Bowling Green with our pints of bitter, that Mary said, 'Wasn't that a lovely day, Spike? Have you ever thought that you'd like to live in the country?'

I said, 'I wouldn't mind it at all, I'm getting a bit fed up with London. What about you?'

She said, 'Yes, I think I'd like a change. How would we go about it?'

'Supposing,' I said brightly, 'supposing I was to get a job on a farm, a job with a cottage thrown in? I was reading somewhere that if you work on a farm they have to give you a cottage.'

'Do you think you could do farm work Spike?' she asked with all the naivety of youth. Mary was ten years younger than me, and still is.

'Could I do it? Of course I could do it,' I scoffed, with all the self assurance of a fully matured thirty-one-year-old idiot.

Three weeks later with our worldly belongings taking up a small corner of a small furniture van, a dog that we had erroneously rescued from the Battersea Dogs' Home, and a month's rent belonging to the landlord, we set forth for Manor Farm, near Nowhere, Buckinghamshire.

I was now a Ministry of Agriculture student on an ex-serviceman's grant of four pounds a week, less two shillings for the use of the ex-war department furniture on loan for the tied cottage attached to the farm where I was to learn my new trade of Farm Management, eventually perhaps to become a farm bailiff. The term 'farm bailiff' had appealed to me very much when the local organizer, one Captain Payne, had mentioned it during the interview in his little Ministry of Agriculture office in Aylesbury.

I don't know why I'd chosen Aylesbury to make my preliminary enquiries. Perhaps I thought I'd get a job on an Aylesbury duck farm. And duck farming must be better than cow farming. I was frightened of cows but I wasn't frightened of ducks. I wasn't too sure what farm bailiffs did. But I somehow imagined myself swaggering around in a Norfolk jacket and jodhpurs, complete with riding crop, giving the yokels a hard time and having first nights with freshly married village virgins, although not really certain if it was the squire or the bailiff who had that honour, but we'll cross that hurdle when we come to it.

CHAPTER 13

John Frost is in my memory the epitome of an English farmer. Physically, a square man with bow legs, he stood four square and miserable against the slings and arrows of outrageous fortune and the elements which, winter and summer, were sent to bankrupt him.

Every morning of his life, except Sundays which he set aside to pray for the idiots who worked for him, he collected his cap, stick and dog, and stomped out of his house into his farmyard to bear witness to his own ruination. Farm carts that had served his father and, aye, his father's father, fell to pieces before his eyes. Tractors that had been bought in good faith as being in 'working order' not twenty years ago, ground their own guts into metallic rubbish just to prove how the vendor, now long since dead and beyond justice, had tricked him.

Cows on which he had lavished care, and indeed affection, such as is not often seen in these parts twixt a man and his beasts, came to the milking shed only to eat his priceless cattlecake and pass wind through their udders, without a thought as to what was to become of us without the weekly milk cheque, while their young, every one a bullcalf, husked themselves to death in the barn.

He had but to raise his eyes from where the sow would soon be lying on her suffocated piglets to see up the meadow, past where his crops were rotting in the ground, to his sheep huddled together in the only flooded patch inviting foot rot while they waited to abort.

His hen-faced wife, her steel hair hammered into a bun at the nape of her carbolic neck, and her black dress freshly blacked, sold milk each morning at her kitchen door to the village wives, and was famous for her short measures, short change and short answers.

The cottage they allocated to us had been built some time in the seventeenth century and redecorated and modernized some time in the eighteenth century.

The Ministry furniture, a trestle table, four kitchen chairs and two canvas folding chairs of the type normally seen on film sets or safaris, added to the odd bits and pieces we ourselves had collected, just about furnished the stone paved kitchen, leaving the rest of the house empty, save for our double bed in the front room.

The dog, a medium sized mongrel bitch that was to guard us against rats, intruders, mad bulls, mad cows, or any other perils that might beset us in this strange land, quickly set out to endorse the sagacity of her previous owners when they had taken her to Battersea Dogs' Home, probably to be put down. The sight of almost any farm animal sent her stiff-legged, shivering with fear, until the time came when she only moved off the old blanket in the kitchen, where she slept day and night dreaming whimpering dreams, to answer the calls of nature outside the back door as near to the step as possible.

Taking her for a walk to introduce her to the beauties of the English countryside, in the hope that she might pluck up courage and catch a rabbit for dinner, meant dragging her along until either her collar came off or the string broke, when she would bolt for home with a turn of speed that would have made her at least a second favourite at Harringay Dog Track any night of the week.

Mary and I had regular arguments about that dog which often got out of all proportion to the subject. I'd be sitting at the table after tea reading the *Daily Mirror* or the latest Ministry text book on pig rearing. You had to sit at the table to read to get the full benefit of the light from the oil lamp. The dog would be curled on her blanket fretfully yapping and whimpering through one of her incessant nightmares.

'I'm going to borrow a gun and shoot that dog tomorrow. Old Shep said he'd shoot it, if it was his.'

'You're always saying that, and anyway it's not Shep's dog so he can't shoot it, and neither can you, so there.'

'Reg the cowman's terrier caught two rabbits up the cornfield yesterday.'

'Well get yourself a terrier, you're not going to shoot Trixie.'

'That dog is useless, all it does is eat and sleep, and it can't even sleep properly. It's a four-legged ponce on me.'

'She can't be a ponce, she's a lady dog and you can't have lady ponces. Although you might know better having spent half your life in that sort of company.'

'What's all that got to do with the dog?'

'I don't know, but it's true, and I find the subject tasteless and boring so let's leave it, shall we?'

I never won.

In the beginning there were all sorts of surprises.

One lunchtime I went home and Mary said, 'There's no milk for tea I'm afraid, I haven't had time to go up to the farm for a second lot and I dropped the first lot when I was – er – I was chased.'

'Who chased you? I'll kill him.'

'It wasn't a him, it was a – er – a pig.'

'A pig!? You can't get chased by a pig. You're sure it was a pig? Long fat things with snouts.'

'Of course I know it was a pig, it chased me up the garden and I just got inside the house in time.'

'Perhaps it just wanted to be friends, they say that pigs are easily domesticated, they take to people.'

She was getting annoyed now.

'Look, Clever Dick, I know when I'm being chased. I simply walked in the front garden with the milk and halfway up the garden there were all these little pigs eating the lettuces, so I picked up a piece of wood and clouted one of them, and this big pig came out of the bushes and went for me.'

'Perhaps he knew you were Jewish.'

'I'm not Jewish, I'm half Jewish.'

'Well he only chased you halfway, didn't he?'

Suddenly she was near to tears.

'It's not funny Spike, I was frightened. I'm getting fed up with this place. What with being chased by pigs, and having to take the dog and the lamp whenever I go out to the toilet at night because of the rats out there. I'm fed up with rolling my own cigarettes and walking two and a half miles to the pub once a week when we can afford it. I'm fed up with no gas, no electric, no wireless, and no money.'

I said, 'Really, when you put it like that it doesn't sound too bad does it?'

She smiled through her tears, 'Go back to work, you bloody fool,' she said. 'I'll get over it.'

I was working with old Shep mending some fences that afternoon and I told him about Mary's experience with the pig. When I finished I smiled. 'She's got herself in a right old state,' I said, 'I told her not to be silly. Pigs couldn't hurt you, could they Shep?'

His expression became very serious. 'You tell your wife,' he said, 'hit's a good job' – Shep always used h's in funny places – 'hit's a good job she is a good runner, hif the old sow had had her down God knows what would have happened. She was defending her young 'uns.'

I said, 'D'you mean a sow would actually hurt you?'

He said, 'She'll not only hurt you, but hif you stay still long enough, and she's a mind to, she'll start to heat you.'

The thought of my lovely Mary lying there being eaten by pigs filled me with such horror that I had to go back and see if she was all right. I started to walk, then to run, down the field. The farmer coming up in his pony and trap called, 'Where you off to Dennis?'

'I'm going home to see Mary!'

He shouted, 'It's not five o'clock, you can't go now!'

'Can't I? You watch me!'

When I got there I said, 'You're right about them pigs, they eat people.'

She said, 'You certainly know how to push your luck, don't you?'

I have found that whenever you are enjoying yourself, nine times out of ten, someone will come along and spoil it. I was cutting grass with a tractor up the top meadow. All was right with the world. The sun was shining, bunny rabbits were bobbing about, a kestrel was keeping me company overhead, when the farmer appeared.

'I think you'd better start giving Reg a hand with the milking Dennis. You'll find him in the milking shed somewhere between half past five and six o'clock tomorrow morning, is that all right?'

'Yes Mr Frost, that's OK.'

'You can go home to your breakfast about half eight when you've got 'em turned out again. Old Reg will soon put you right. He's a good cowman is Reg, a bit crotchety at times but a good cowman.'

Reg was a tall rangy man with a round red country face about two sizes too small for him, which looked like an apple with a cap on it. He had told me while we were making silage that he'd been a cowman all his life, almost as far back as he could remember, and he hated the sight of 'the dratted beasts'.

The cows were bunched up round the gate behind the shed when I passed at about six o'clock the next morning. *En masse* in the half light they looked a lot more menacing than they did individually, eating buttercups down the field in the sunshine. And when I looked at those horns I wished I'd said that I didn't want to learn about cattle, only sheep, and ducks.

Reg was clanking about with buckets and other milking paraphernalia as I entered the shed.

'Mornin' Reg.'

'Mornin' Dennis.'

It's funny that once people start off calling me Dennis they seldom accept Spike.

The milking shed is very bleak, cold and unfriendly, with its concrete floor and empty stalls lit by naked light bulbs hanging from the rafters.

'What do you want me to do, Reg?'

190

'It's all right, I've done it all now, I've been here since half past five.'

Well good for you mate!

He plonks a bucket of water down and tosses a couple of pieces of rag into it. 'I'll go and let 'em in.' Then he clumps out through the open doors at the end of the shed, disappearing round the corner, along the path to the field.

Standing there in the empty silent shed I can think of a lot of places I'd sooner be. A rat scuttles along the floor by the wall and makes me jump. If there's anything that frightens me as much as cows it's rats. They say that cows are harmless creatures, well if they are so harmless why have they got those bloody great horns on their heads? For two pins I'd go home again and get back into bed with Mary, which is much more sensible than standing here waiting to be gored to death.

The cows when they come, come not as a thundering herd, but softly, pitapat, shyly, like visitors.

The first four are in the door before they notice me, and then they stop and look. A big black and white one puts her head up and bellows. If I make a run for the door at the other end they'll have me before I've got more than a few yards, and even then it might be locked. There's a pitchfork leaning against the wall if I can reach it. Apparently disconcerted by my sudden movement, all the front cows turn and they try to force their way back through the others behind them.

Reg's voice can be heard shouting angrily, 'Go on! Git in there! What's the matter with you, you stupid animals?' He appears round the corner wading waist deep in cows.

191

'Don't stand there waving that pitchfork Dennis, you're frightening 'em.'

Reassured by the presence of the expert, and the fact that they can be frightened, I put down the pitchfork and nonchalantly press myself to the wall as they pass, quietly taking their places in the stalls. Reg starts tethering each one in turn with a chain round its neck.

'What was that two tine fork for? You ain't afraid of a few old cows, are you Dennis?'

I said, 'Well, I've never been this close to any cows before, and you sort of don't know what to expect, do you?'

He slaps the cow he is securing a resounding blow on the flank. 'They won't hurt you boy.' And to the cow, 'We won't hurt old Dennis there, will we Rosie?'

The cow gives a little 'moo' which I couldn't accept as a definite 'No.' His attention is attracted by something behind me. The big black and white cow that frightened me is standing in the stall, and another cow, a red one, is trying to get in there as well.

'Doris!' Reg roars, 'Get out of there, you contrary old bitch! Get her out of there Dennis, she's in the wrong stall and she knows she is, go on, get her out, the Friesian, the black and white one!'

Get her out of there! How to get her out of there? Approaching cautiously, 'Come on,' I say, with timid authority. 'Come on out!'

'Not like that!' shouts Reg, his apple face going purple. 'Get round the front of her! Look, I'll show you, like this!'

He picks up a wooden three-legged milking stool by the leg and waving it above his head forces his way past the two animals, shouting, 'I'll teach you, you

192

dratted idiots. You're really mucking me about this morning, ain't you?' And having reached a position where he is now facing the cows, he gives them both, innocent and guilty, a clonking blow on the head with the stool. The animals shy backwards, one of them slips and nearly falls, and in a moment all the cows that have not been chained mill about, bellowing and evacuating their bowels, as cows apparently do when they are frightened.

Reg has gone berserk and wades into them almost blue faced, shouting oaths, and lashing out in all directions with his stool. His feet slip from under him on the slimy green that now covers the concrete floor, and he disappears in the lowing, slipping, scrambling, wild eyed mass. His hand still waving the stool is the last part of him to disappear, like a man in animal quicksand.

I have a brief momentary thought of attempting a rescue, but it soon passes with the reasoning that one life is enough to lose in one morning. Just as he went he reappears, slowly, minus the stool, one hand gripping a tossing horn and the other over another animal's back, his coat is spattered with cow dung and his face is contorted with pain. Using cows as crutches he limps over to the nearest stall, clutching his ankle.

'Dratted animals,' he grunts, 'one of them kicked me in the ankle, that do smart that do.'

The cows, now left to their own devices, go quietly back into their stalls.

'You see that bucket, Dennis?'

'Yes.'

'There's a bit of rag in the water, get the rag and go along after me and wash their bags off, can you do that?'

193

'What bags?'

'The udders boy, the teats!'

Taking a deep breath, the cold wet piece of rag in one hand, the bucket in the other, I approach the first cow in the line as quietly as an Apache creeping up on General Custer. Slowly I put a hand under the animal and a hoof flashes forward knocking me and the bucket in a sprawling clattering heap to the other side of her front legs. Picking myself up and holding the back of my thigh where she caught me, I cautiously limp to safety.

Reg limps over carrying in each hand an Alfa Lavel milking churn with their clusters of pipes and fitments. We haven't been here half an hour yet and we're both injured. Where's it all going to end?

'I thought you said these things were harmless? And don't tell me I frightened her. I was as quiet as a sodding mouse.'

'Ar, that's where you went wrong Dennis, you frightened her because you were too quiet. How would you like someone creeping up and suddenly putting a cold wet rag on your tits?'

'I haven't got any tits, and I won't have any bloody legs either if I keep this lark up much longer.'

His little windfall of a face creases to a smile. 'You've got to talk to 'em, look, I'll show you.'

He goes over to the cow that has just kicked me and is now back to munching the cattlecake in her trough, as if nothing had happened.

'Come on over girl, git over,' he says quietly and puts his hand on her rump giving a little push. The cow looks round and carries on munching.

'Now she knows I'm here and I've come to milk her, got that Dennis?'

194

'I've got it.'

He plugs the milking apparatus into the system and puts each one of the cups on to a teat tying a piece of cord over the animal's back to secure them. As he does so the leg twitches, I hope she kicks him.

'She is a bit touchy,' he says, 'I think she's got a touch of mastitis. See that lump on her bag?'

I look and nod without any great interest.

'That's what we call mastitis.'

'What do you do, call the vet?'

'We might have to. I'll give it a little bit of my own treatment and we'll see how she is tomorrow.'

Standing on one of the rails of a stall, he searches the oak beams above.

'It's here somewhere. I put it up here out of the way of the rats. Here it is.'

He returns to earth holding a dirty greyish object roughly the size and shape of a tennis ball.

'Goose grease, my old father used to swear by goose grease.'

He turns it in his hand and indicates some little tooth shaped dents. 'Them dratted rats have been at it, you can't hide anything from 'em, that you can't.'

Bending down under the animal he rubs the ball of grease against the lump on the udder for a few moments, then straightens up. 'That'll probably do it. That vet don't know everything. He don't know about goose grease and I'm not going to tell him. Now let's get on. Talk to 'em, let 'em know you're there, they won't hurt you.'

I continued wiping the leathery teats. 'Come on, git over girl!' A pat on the rump, it was easy, until, 'Come on, git over girl.' A pat on the rump and, Crash! I'm up in the corner again.

'What did I do wrong there?'

'Ar, that's old Buttercup, she's always been a bit jumpy. We always tie her leg. I forgot to tell you about her.'

'Well thanks very much.'

'That's all right Dennis, you're getting on well boy, we'll make a cowman of you yet.'

'If I live that long.'

When we'd finished milking with the machines he showed me how to strip off the remaining milk from the cow sitting on a stool in the traditional manner.

'That's right Dennis, not too hard, a nice rhythm. Keep your shoulder into her leg so she can't kick you if you're a bit clumsy at first.'

By the time I got round to Buttercup, the one who upended me just for fun, I'd got the hang of it. 'Git over girl.' A pat on the rump. Make certain her leg is tied, put my shoulder against it, just in case. Nothing can happen now. A tail with a foot long tassel of filth at the end of it hits me across the face like a whip.

Steady Mullins, think about the bailiff's job and the village virgins!

So life goes on, cows to be milked morning and afternoon, hay making to do, and pigs to be fed, sheep to be dipped, a sow to be ringed to stop her rooting her sty to pieces. There are heifers to be held for the vet, a slipping sliding bruising job, the vet in his white coat leaning nonchalant and unhurried over the half door of the barn while two of us drag each kicking, hooking, wild eyed animal, hanging on to her horns, two fingers in her snotty nostrils, until she's close enough for him to insert a syringe in her neck without exerting himself.

196

'Do you think you could reach over a bit more, sir? We can't hold this one.'

'Don't talk to the vet like that Dennis, Mr Thomas knows what he's doing. Now get hold of her, she's only a baby.'

The harvest comes, the yellow corn to be piled in stooks from the binder. The last stand of corn in the centre of the field is seething with rabbits. The guns are out, popping them off as they break cover. Two foxes break and go lolloping away to the far hedge.

'Don't shoot them foxes,' shouts the farmer, 'let 'em go, the Hunt can have them!'

'Don't you think that's cruel,' I ask, 'saving them to be torn to pieces by a pack of dogs instead of shooting 'em?'

He shakes his head slowly and looks at me pityingly. 'Dennis,' he says, 'you townspeople have got a lot to learn, haven't you?'

'Well it seems obvious to me . . .'

Another slow shake of the head.

'Now listen Dennis, the chance of any of those guns bringing down one of those foxes while they are going away is very unlikely. But they'll hit 'em with a few pellets, and next week we'll find an old fox somewhere, probably still alive, being eaten to death by maggots. Which is kinder, that, or being killed in five seconds by a pack of hounds?'

Could it be Mr Frost has a heart under that tweed waistcoat, or am I being whitewashed?

The harvest ended, one evening Mrs Frost stopped me on the way home to hand me a small parcel.

'Mr Mullins! I want you to give these groceries to your wife.'

The thought of La Frost giving somebody some-

197

thing for nothing was too much for me, and she perceived that I was going into shock.

'It's your share of the rations for the harvest home supper.'

'What's that?'

I didn't think she could be embarrassed, but she was; she looked around the farmyard for a distraction and rattled the bunch of keys that hung from her waist.

'Well, er, it's a country tradition to give a supper for the hands when the harvest is in, but we don't go in for that sort of thing at this farm, so there is your share of the extra rations we are allowed for the occasion.'

'Well, thanks very much.'

I wouldn't want to go to a party with this needle nosed old bitch anyway.

'Thank you Mrs Frost.'

'That's all right Mr Mullins, your wife can pay me when she calls for the milk in the morning.'

Cow!

Autumn came, the autumn leaves, tinted glorious shades of red and gold, blocked the gutter and the rain flooded the front room where the bed was. Mary found it harder to gather dry wood to start the fire each morning in the great head-high oak-beamed fireplace in the kitchen. We sat there in the evenings surrounded by drying twigs, and went to bed apprehensive that a spark would burn the house down, or perhaps hoping that it would.

The fields turned grey, and even the beasts seemed affected by the hopelessness of winter. Cows came wet and miserable to the milking, and Reg reacted to their petty quarrels more vehemently than ever. Even old Rose the Ayrshire, who always got from me a secret extra handful of cattlecake because she was always so good, never kicked the bucket over or tossed her head while being chained, now stayed down the field at milking time until I'd walked a quarter of a mile through whipping wet grass in the morning mist to find her. You expected such childishness from Starr or Vera, but not from Rosie.

One evening in November when we were sitting there by our spluttering fire surrounded by our steaming twigs and the room bathed in the warm glow of the stinking oil lamp, Mary said, 'Do you know something, Spike? I was looking at that picture today,' she pointed to a print we'd once bought from the National Gallery of Constable's 'Cornfield' hanging over the fireplace, 'and in the knowledge that I've acquired in the last few months I've got a whole new angle on that scene.'

'What d'you mean?'

'Well, take that farmer's boy, who we always thought had thrown himself down to drink from the sparkling brook. I now know that what really happened is that he has collapsed from rickets, overwork and starvation, with perhaps a touch of cowpox. And he is looking in the water contemplating suicide, or would it be infanticide? And those sheep have all got the tick, warble fly, liver fluke, and foot rot, most of which they've passed on to the old shepherd to go with his piles and rheumatism that he got sitting under wet hedges in the rain having his cold tea and sandwiches, just like you do sometimes. Spike, let's go home.'

Ah well, I never really did believe that stuff about the bailiff and the village virgins, anyway.

199

CHAPTER 14

Back in London we stayed in a council flat in Brixton long enough to have our two boys, Kennedy and Kevin, moving eventually to a little terraced house in Slough where we still live at the time of writing.

On the whole, life was good to us. We never had too much of anything but we got by with me working at whatever came along, just as I had always done. In turn, I worked as a steel erector, a builder's labourer, a barman, a shop assistant, a deck hand on a dredger, and other jobs either too brief in duration to remember or to be worth mentioning. Chargehands in the factories I tried were generally the sharpest at recognizing a misfit when they saw one, and in some cases I left the production line and was on my way before I even found out what we were making.

Steel erecting was a well-paid, convivial way to make a living. But, alas, that came to an end when something went wrong and I almost fell off the top of Harringay Arena. Whereupon, there and then, I promised God that if He got me down safely I would never climb anything higher than a step ladder; a promise I have faithfully kept to this day with no difficulty whatsoever.

House painting I enjoyed as much as one can enjoy honest toil, but that often terminated soon after the employer found out I wasn't a house painter. Whereas general labouring on building sites, although harder and dirtier, was less fraught with peril, because once you mastered the wheelbarrow and the shovel, and got some clay on your boots, all you had to do was blend in with the general confusion.

In fact it was as a general labourer during the building of the Festival of Britain Funfair in Battersea Park that I enjoyed my greatest triumph by becoming an official, a trade union shop steward, a representative of the Union of Transport and General Workers. Although I must admit that I became a shop steward not from any great interest in the needs of poor bloody suffering humanity, but simply because nobody else among the Irish labourers, spivs, criminals and general deadbeats on my section of the site wanted the job.

Once elected to office I laboured no more, but sat each day in a hut with the other shop stewards, all of us drunk with power, imbibing tea, reading newspapers, and working out our overtime, with just an occasional reconnaissance outside to ascertain that our brothers, leaning on their picks and shovels, or playing 'Two up' in quiet corners when they weren't in the nearest pub getting drunk, were not being downtrodden and oppressed by the oppressor who paid our wages.

Throughout this time I don't think I ever actually gave up the idea that one day I would become a writer. Although at times it did occur to me that it was a pity I had to prove myself a failure at almost everything that everybody else did for a living before somebody recognized me as such. I wrote stories, articles and playlets, which I either threw away when they were finished, or sent to publishers or producers and threw away when they came back. It was always disappointing, but life, caring for a family with two growing boys, was often too busy to worry about it for very long. There were lizards to be caught on Burnham Beeches, aquariums to be made, aeroplanes to be assembled and crashed on Christmas morning. There were mice to be caged, school reports to be frowned on, gramophone records to be intolerated, dirty books and cigarette ends to be discovered, and headmasters to be had a word with.

It was not to be until one January morning in 1963 that a chance remark made by one of a gang of painters with whom I was allegedly painting some houses at Gerrards Cross was to actually start me on the road, often bumpy but always exciting, to whatever success I enjoy as a writer. I was feeling particularly disenchanted that morning. Some stories I had sent to a literary agent in high hopes had been returned with a note to the effect that he liked them but they were 'too grass roots' for any publisher he could think of. What the hell is 'too grass roots'? It can't mean dirty. I never wrote a dirty story in my life.

So on the morning in question, we were seated around the kitchen of an empty house drinking our flasks of tea, eating our sandwiches and reading our papers, when one of our number, a young man by the name of Brian Goom, said, 'Here Spike, it says here in *Reveille* that Max Bygraves is looking for writers to be trained in writing for television. You were telling me that you do a bit of writing, why don't you have a go?'

I said, 'No thanks Brian, I'm getting fed up with that lark. I've come to the conclusion it's a waste of time, so I've decided to dedicate my life to painting walls and windows.'

The old foreman looked up from his *Daily Mirror.* 'I'm glad you didn't say ceilings,' he growled; 'those ceilings in number twenty-seven are a bloody mess, I've just had a look at 'em.'

Oh blimey, don't say I'm going to get the sack again, so soon after Christmas!

When I was leaving to go home that night I picked up the magazine Brian had quoted and took it with me. After tea that evening, I showed the article to Mary, who immediately said, 'There's no argument Spike, you've got to have a go, haven't you? I'll never get a mink coat with the money you're earning as a painter, will I now?'

I said, 'You might think this is a poor excuse not to keep banging my head against that particular wall, but to be honest I don't think a mink coat would suit you love.'

She said, 'Well don't let that worry you, mate, because I don't want to wear it, I want to drag it along the ground behind me. So stop bellyaching and get writing.'

When the kids had gone to bed we worked until about two o'clock in the morning, me writing in longhand and Mary typing the words on our old three quid typewriter, as we still do, only the typewriter has changed. When we'd finished we had a monologue to go with the song 'A Shanty in Old Shanty Town.' And a few pages of another idea which for the life of me I can't remember. The next morning we posted it off and pretended to forget all about it, as we always did.

Three days later an envelope dropped on to the mat containing a cheque and the letter reproduced here:

MB/PE   29th January 1963

Dear Spike Mullins,
Many thanks for the script received
this morning, and I am elated with the way you
wrote this. Of course it is not all usable
but I think a good 40% or 50% is, which is
wonderful from a seven page script. So as you
will not think you are wasting your time, I enclose
a cheque for £25.0.0d on account of the script I will
get when I have spoken to you and just
given you a few more outlets for the comedy.
Thank you once again for your kind interest.

Most sincerely,
Patricia Ebdon
Dictated by Mr Bygraves and
Signed in his absence

A week later Max invited me to go to Nottingham to
see his show and to get an idea what it was all about.
Then after the show he said, 'Spike, I'm going out for a
meal with a couple of friends, Sid James and his wife,
would you like to come along?' I would have loved to
have said, 'No thanks, I've had enough excitement for
one day.' But if I'd chickened out Mary would never
have forgiven me.
   So, half an hour later, there I was, sitting at a table
sparkling with untouchable glass and cutlery, too
terrified to eat anything, drinking gin and tonic,
which I hate, because it seemed the right thing to do,
and hoping I was the only one who could hear my

stomach rumbling. I couldn't eat now, even if I wanted to, because the waiter had taken all my knives and forks away.

I gazed around at all the beautiful people, eating their fabulous food, served to them by immaculate waiters. Then back to my own situation, on my right the legendary Sid James, on my left his lovely wife Valerie, and opposite, my new employer Max Bygraves. And the thought occurred to me that so often in my life I've had to say to myself, 'Mullins, you got yourself into this, now get yourself out of it.'

But this time I said, 'Mullins, you got yourself into this, now try and stay in it.'

That was sixteen years ago, and I think I'm winning. But that, as they say, is another story.

This identity certificate is intended for use on successive voyages, BUT it will be necessary on each new engagement to fill in one of the series of small pages inside the certificate. The front and back pages should not require alteration.

ARGENTINE IMMIGRATION REGULATIONS.

FICHA INDIVIDUAL.
IDENTIFICATION CERTIFICATE

MARINA MERCANTE INGLESA.
BRITISH MERCANTILE MARINE.

Ficha del tripulante ..... *DENNIS MULLINS*
Full Name of Seaman

Nacionalidad *INGLESA* edad *19* años
Nationality *Age* *Years*

Hijo de ..... *JOSEPH* ..... y de ..... *EDITH*
Name of Father *Name of Mother*

Estado civil? ..... *S* ..... sabe leer? *Si* ..... sabe escribir? *Si*
Single or Married *Able to read* *Able to write*

Estatura ..... *1* ..... m ..... *75* ..... cent .....
Height *metres* *centimetres*

Color del cabello ..... *RUBIO*
Colour of Hair

Nariz (chica, grande, regular, recta, etc.) *REGULAR*
Nose (small, large, regular, square, etc.)

Color de ojos *AZULES* color de piel *BLANCO*
Colour of Eyes *Complexion*